THE BIG FRENCH VOCABULARY WORKBOOK

Boost your French with OVER 1000 WORDS!

La table des matières / Table of contents

Want to learn more? Check out our other language learning books an Amazon!

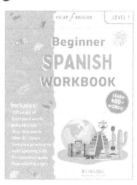

Beginner French Phrases   Beginner French Workbook   Beginner Spanish Workbook

INTRODUCTION

Bonjour and welcome to your new Vocabulary workbook!

We applaud you for learning a new language! It is a challenging yet rewarding goal! Successfully learning a new language, requires many important steps such as learning grammar, conjugation, extensive listening, many (often uncomfortable) conversation practice, and...**building a wide range of vocabulary**! This workbook was designed exactly for that purpose! To help you increase your French vocabulary quickly and efficiently. Each word is accompanied by a picture, its name in English and French, including articles to help you figure out noun genders (very important in French) as well as its pronunciation.

Fun exercises and quizzes will help you review more actively to improve memorization. This workbook is sure to be a great addition to your language material.

Page after page, you will work through close to **1200 useful everyday words in 80 themes**! Tips to help you remember them:

- Take your time! There is no need to rush through the pages, go at your own pace.
- Review your new words from time to time, even after completing the whole book.
- Build flashcards to review them more conveniently.
- Consistency is key. It is preferable to do a little bit everyday than several pages once a week.
- And most importantly: Use your words immediately to help solidify them in your memory. **Make your own simple sentences, speaking with someone or even by yourself.** Try having a little conversation using the vocabulary of each theme or write a small paragraph.

Remember:
Words you don't use are words you'll forget!

We wish you great success in your language learning journey!

The Bilingoal Team

BASICS

≫ __Alphabet and pronunciation__ ≪

The French alphabet is composed of 26 letters: 20 consonants and 6 vowels (a, e, i, o, u, y).

• L'alphabet (lal•fah•beh)

Letter / Pronounced / Sounds like:

A a	ah	a in dad
B b	beh	b in bat
C c	seh	• s before i and e • k with other letters
D d	deh	d in dad
E e	uh	**e** in th**e**
F f	eff	Same as English
G g	jeh	- s in Asia before **e** and **i** - g in **g**as with other vowels
H h	ash	always <u>silent</u> (except in "ch")
I i	ee	**ee** in s**ee** **y** in **y**es (adieu, oeil)
J j	jee	s in Asia
K k	kah	Same as English
L l	el	Softer than in English
M m	em	Same as English

Letter / Pronounced / Sounds like:

N n	en	Same as English
O o	oh	o in orange
P p	peh	• p in pet • pronounced in "psy" words
Q q	qü	• k in koala (qui/que...) • kw in "équa.../aqua..." words
R r	err	trilled sound in the back of mouth (not throat)
S s	ess	Same as English
T t	teh	t in taco
U u *	ü	see below
V v	veh	Same as English
W w	doobl veh	• usually **w** in **w**eekend • **v** in a few words
X x	eeks	Same as English
Y y	ee grek	• **ee** in b**ee**t (la gym) • or **y** in **y**es (les yeux)
Z z	zed	• Usually like English • can be silent (chez, riz)

*

<u>To pronounce letter U</u>: Round your lips into an "O" shape while saying "EE" instead. The U sound is written as **ü** in the guide.

• Accents

There are 4 marks placed on 5 vowels (a, e, i, o, u) and 1 on **C**:

L'accent aigü	L'accent grave	L'accent circonflexe	Le Tréma	La cédille
´	`	^	¨	ç
e (uh) ⇒ é (eh)	e ⇒ è (ay)	(â, ê, î, ô, û)	(ë, ï, ü)	ç
• makes **e (uh)** sound like **(eh): é**	• also modifies meaning of words: ou (or) - o**ù** (where)	• opens and lengthens the vowels • indicates that a letter was removed (from latin)	• a vowel with "tréma" must be pronounced as a separate sound not a combined sound	Makes **c** sound like **[s]**

• Combinations

Some letters, when combined make a different sound:

Examples of combinations:	-AU -EAU -OT	words ending in: ER / EZ	EU	GN	ILL
Pronounced:	**oh**	**eh**	**uh**	**nyuh**	**y** in **yes** *
	bateau (bah.toh) [boat]	parler (par.leh) [speak]	beurre (buhr) butter	piña colada	une fille (fee) A girl

*There are exceptions: a city = une ville (veel)

Examples of combinations:	Œ	Oi	OU	TION	QU
Pronounced:	**uh**	**wa**	**oo**	**syoh** (nasal sound)	**k** *
	sœur (suhr) sister	oiseau (wa.zoh) bird	poulet (poo.leh) chicken	nation (nah.syoh) nation	quiche (keesh) quiche

*or **kw** in "Aqua/Équa" words: équation, aquarium...

• **Nasal sounds**

Nasal sounds often occurs when **a vowel is followed by N or M**. (In the pronunciation guide, that nasal sound is written in bold and underlined.)
The best way to learn them is to listen to French and imitate what you hear.

French nasal combinations	Symbol in the guide	Sounds <u>a bit</u> like:
–en, –em, –an, –am	**-ah**	**on** in s**on**g
–un, –in, –ain, –aim –im	**-uh**	**an** in **an**kle
–on, –om	**-oh**	**on** in b**on**bon
–oin	**-wuh**	**wan** in **wan**gle
–ien	**-yuh**	**yan** in **Yan**kee

(!) <u>CONSONANTS AT THE END OF WORDS ARE OFTEN *NOT* PRONOUNCED IN FRENCH.</u>

This often leads to words with 2 vowel sounds next to each other which the French language is not really fond of. To remedy the situation two things often happen:

 • **"Une Liaison"** (lee.ay.z**oh**)

A "liaison" is linking the pronunciation between to words, usually in words **ending in s** (also **t, d, r, n**) followed by a word **starting with a vowel**.
Note that **S** is pronounced like a **Z** in that case.

Ex: The friends = Le**s a**mis (leh zah.mee) A friend = U**n a**mi (**uh** nah.mee)

 • **Une Élision** (eh.lee.zy**oh**)

Another change that can happen is a contraction called élision. It makes the language more fluid and easier to pronounce.

Ex: • The friend = L'ami (lah.mee) <u>NOT</u> Le ami

• The man = L'homme (lom) <u>NOT</u> Le homme (h is silent)

• Articles

Nouns (people, places, things) are either singular or plural but unlike English are either feminine or masculine. Articles (the, a, an) vary depending on the gender and number. Learning new words with their article can help you remember their gender which is important since other words (like adjectives...) must agree with the noun they modify.

	DEFINITE ARTICLES: **THE**		INDEFINITE ARTICLES: **A/AN (SOME)**	
	singular	**plural**	**singular**	**plural**
MASCULINE	le / l' *	les (leh)	un	des
FEMININE	la / l' *	les	une	des
	Le téléphone (m.) , la télévision (f.) Les téléphones (pural)		Un téléphone (m.) , Une télévision (f.) Des télévisions (pl.)	

* **Le** or **La** become **L'** when followed by a noun starting with **a vowel** and some words starting with **h.**

≫ <u>Conjugation</u> ≪

• Verb facts:

• **Verbs** can be: • Regular: Always follow a conjugation pattern

  • Irregular: Do not follow a pattern or have an irregular root (stem).

• **Infinitive:** A verb in the infinitive, the "to" form (**To** sleep) in French are divided into 3 groups, defined by their ending. The -ER, -IR or -RE group.

• **Stem:** A verb in French is composed of a stem (also called "root") and an ending. The stem is the verb without the infinitive ending (-er, -ir, -re).

  Ex: • To speak = Parler   (Stem: **parl**.   Ending: **er**)

• Each group follows a specific conjugation pattern.

• To conjugate a (regular) verb, the ending (-er, -ir, -re) is dropped and a new ending specific to the subject is added. The most important tenses to know as a beginner are: the present, compound past, imperfect and future for regular vebs and the most common irregular verbs. Let's review them for regular verbs.

• Subject pronouns

SINGULAR	I	**Je / J'**
	you (informal)	**Tu**
	he / she / we (informal)	**il / elle / on**
PLURAL	we (formal)	**nous**
	you (formal or to a group)	**vous**
	They (masc. / fem.)	**ils / elles**

- **Je** becomes **J'** if followed by a vowel.

- "Tu" is used only with someone you are familiar with (friend, family member...), or between teens/kids.

- In a formal setting use "vous" instead of "tu". **Vous** also means "you" when talking to a group.

- "On" is an informal "we", very common in everyday speech.

•To be / To have
Two important irregular verbs to master:

• To be (Present tense) • Être

I am	je **suis**	(süee)
you are (inf.)	tu **es**	(ay)
he / she / we are (inf.)	il / elle / on **est**	(ay)/(**oh**.nay)
we are (form.)	nous **sommes**	(som)
you are	vous **êtes**	(voo zet)
they are	ils / elles **sont**	(s**oh**)

• To have (Present tense) • Avoir

I have	j'**ai**	(jay)
you have (inf.)	tu **as**	(ah)
he / she has/ we have (inf.)	il / elle / on **a**	(ah)/**oh**.nah)
we have (form.)	nous **avons**	(noo zah.v**oh**)
you have	vous **avez**	(voo zah.veh)
they have	ils / elles **ont**	(eel z**oh**)

(Did you notice the many "liaisons" in the pronunciation?)

Present tense

For regular verbs. Remember, remove ending (-er, –ir, -re) and add:

	-ER	-IR	-RE
Je	-e	-is	-s
Tu	-es	-is	-s
Il / Elle / On	-e	-it	stem only
Nous	-ons	-issons	-ons
Vous	-ez	-issez	-ez
Ils / Elles	-ent	-issent	-ent

Ex: • Speak = Parler (stem: **parl**) Je parle, tu parles, nous parlons ....

    • Finish = Finir (stem: **fin**): Je finis, il finit, vous finissez ...

    • Lose = Perdre (stem: **perd**): Je perds, elle perd, ils perdent

The Imperfect

L'imparfait is used to describe something that was ongoing or repeated in the past, something that you "used to" do, or that used to happen...
Remove the infinitive endings and replace with:

	-ER	-IR	-RE
Je	-ais	-issais	-ais
Tu	-ais	-issais	-ais
Il / Elle / On	-ait	-issait	-ait
Nous	-ions	-issions	-ions
Vous	-iez	-issiez	-iez
Ils / Elles	-aient	-issaient	-aient

Ex: • I used to speak/ I was speaking: Je parl**ais** (pahr.lay)

    • You were finishing/ used to finish: Tu fin**issais** (fee.nee.say)

    • They were losing: Ils perd**aient** (pair.day)

The Coumpound past

Called "**Le passé composé**", it is the most used past tense, often alongside the "Imperfect".
Called coumpound (or composé) because it is composed of two verbs, an auxialiary verb,
être (to be) or **avoir** (to have) and a past participle (2nd verb). Most verbs use **avoir**:

• *Passé composé* **with "avoir":**

J'**ai**

Tu **as**

Il / Elle / On **a**

Nous **avons**

Vous **avez**

Ils / Elles **ont**

**Replace verb
ending with:**

-**ER** ⇒ -é

-**IR** ⇒ -i

-**RE** ⇒ -u

<u>**Ex**</u>:

• I spoke / I have spoken / I did speak:

J'ai parl**é** (jay pahr.leh)

• You finished / you have finished...:

Tu as fin**i** (fee.nee)

• We lost / we have lost / we did lose:

Nous Avons perd**u** (noo zah.v**oh** pair.dü)

• **Passé composé with être:**

Similar process but the past participle (2nd verb) must agree with the subject:

Je **suis**

Tu **es**

Il / Elle / On **est**

Nous **sommes**

Vous **êtes**

Ils / Elles s**ont**

**Replace verb
ending with:**

-**ER** ⇒ -é

-**IR** ⇒ -i

-**RE** ⇒ -u

<u>**You must add:**</u>

• -**e** if the subject is feminine

• -**es** if the subject is feminine (fem.)
and plural (plu.)

• -**s** if the subject is plural

<u>**Ex"**</u>: (partir : to leave)

  • je suis part**i** (**masc./sing.**)

  • je suis parti**e** (**fem./ sing.**)

  • ils sont part**is** (**masc./ plu.**)

  • elles sont parti**es** (**fem./ plu.**)

(parti/partie/partis...is pronounced

the same way [pahr.tee])

-About 17 verbs use **être** in the
"passé composé", such as:

Venir (come), aller (go) ...

The Future

nlike the previous tenses, to conjugate in the future, you **do not** drop the ending for -ER nd -IR (-**RE verbs do lose the final -E**). Simply add the following to the infinitive:

-ER / -IR / -RE ⇨ -R

Je	-ai
Tu	-as
Il / Elle / On	-a
Nous	-ons
Vous	-ez
Ils / Elles	-ont

Ex:
- I will speak: Je parler**ai**

  (pahr.luh.ray)
- You (pl.) will finish: Vous finir**ez**

  (fee.nee.reh)
- They (fem.) will lose: Elles perd**ront**

  (pair.dr**oh**)

≫ Irregular verbs ≪

FIND A USEFUL LIST OF THE MOST COMMON IRREGULAR VERBS AND THEIR CONJUGATION AT THE END OF THE BOOK.

≫ Adjectives ≪

French, the ending of an adjectives must indicate the noun's gender and number. If a noun preceded by: **le** or **un**, it is masculine; **la** or **une**, it is feminine, **Les** and **des** means that the oun is in the plural form. Most adjectives take an -**e** in the feminine and/or an -**s** in the ural. For other adjectives (there are exceptions):

	Adjectives ending in:			
	-E	**-S**	**-F**	**-EUX**
Masc. Sing.	No change	No change	No change	No change
Fem. Sing.	No change	Add -**e**	-**f** becomes -**ve**	-**x** becomes -**se**
Masc. Plur.	Add -**s**	No change	Add -**s**	No change
Fem. Plur.	Add -**s**	Add -**es**	-**f** becomes -**ves**	-**x** becomes -**ses**

• All the adjectives in this book are presented in their masculine and feminine form.

Basic Words & Greetings

There are two ways of talking in French, formally (form.) and informally (inf.). People speak more proper, polite way with older people, people they don't know, or in formal settings (with a teacher, at work, at the bank, store...
• The use of "vous" (you) between 2 people indicates that the conversation is more formal. It's preferable to choose **vous**, unless the speaker adresses you using **tu**.
• **Tu** (you, inf.) is used between friends, family, people who are familiar with each other (of all ages). It is always used between kids and teens (familiar or not). **Tu** is used when talking to one person, **vous** (you. plur) is used when talking to 2 or more people (formally or not). This formal and informal way of talking is also reflected in some greetings and other words.

- Hello   *(Greeting)*
  Bonjour! (b**oh**.joor)
- Hi!
  Salut! (sah.lü)
- Good evening! *(Greeting)*
  Bonsoir! (b**oh**.swahr)
- Good night   *(Farewell)*
  Bonne nuit (bon nüee)
- Good day!   *(Farewell)*
  Bonne journée! (bon joor.neh)
- Good evening! *(Farewell)*
  Bonne soirée! (bon swah.reh)
- Goodbye!
  Au revoir (oh ruh.vwahr)
- Bye!
  Salut! (sah.lü)
- See you (soon)!
  À bientôt! (ah by**uh**.toh)
- See you later!
  À plus tard! (ah plü tahr)

- How are you? (form. or to group)
  Comment-allez vous?
  (koh.m**ah** tah.leh voo)
- How are you? (inf.)
  Comment vas-tu? or Ça va?
  (koh.m**ah** vah tü / sah vah)
- Good
  Bien (by**uh**)
- Very good
  Très bien (tray by**uh**)
- Not bad
  Pas mal (pah.mal)
- Not very good
  Pas très bien (pah tray by**uh**)
- Nice to meet you
  Enchanté(e) (**ah**.sh**ah**.teh)
- Please (form.)
  S'il vous plaît (seel voo play)
- Please (inf.)
  S'il te plaît (seel tuh play)
- Excuse me (form.)
  Excusez-moi (ex.kü.zeh mwah)
- Excuse me (inf.)
  Excuse-moi (ex.küz mwah)

- Sorry!
  Pardon! (pahr.d**oh**)
- Yes / No
  Oui/ Non (wee/n**oh**)
- Maybe
  Peut-être (puh.tetr)
- Of course!
  Bien sûr (by**uh** sür)
- Alright!
  D'accord (dah.kor)
- Thank you (very much)
  Merci (beaucoup)
  (mair.see boh.koo)
- You're welcome
  De rien (duh ry**uh**)

LET'S START!

La famille - Family

Le grand-père

gr**ah**.pair   grandfather

La grand-mère

gr**ah**.mair   grandmother

La mère

mair   mother

Le père

pair   father

Le fils

feess   son

La fille

fee   daughter

Le frère

frair   brother

La soeur

suhr   sister

L'oncle

oh.kl   uncle

La tante

t**ah**t   aunt

Le neveu

nuh.vuh   nephew

La nièce

nyess   niece

➤ Connect each English word to its correct translation:

The sister •	L'oncle
The mother •	La soeur
The brother •	Le grand-père
The uncle •	Le frère
The grandfather •	La mère
The aunt •	La famille
The nephew •	Le père
The father •	Le fils
The daughter •	La grand-mère
The grandmother •	Le neveu
The niece •	La tante
The son •	La fille
The family •	La nièce

⟳ Translate: By memory only first, then fill in any missing words with help from the previous page.

The brother

The sister   The family   The grandmother

The daughter   The grandfather   The niece

The nephew   The mother   The uncle

The father   The son   The aunt

La famille (Extra) - Family (extra)

Le cousin

koo.z**uh**   cousin (m.)

La cousine

koo.zeen   cousin (fem.)

La petite-fille

puh.teet fee granddaughter

Le petit-fils

puh.tee feess   grandson

Moi

mwah   me

La belle-famille

bel fah.mee   In-laws

Le beau-père

boh pair   father-in-law

La belle-mère

bel mair   mother-in-law

Le beau-frère

boh frair   brother-in-law

La belle-soeur

bel suhr   sister-in-law

Le beau-fils

boh feess   son-in-law

La belle-fille

bel fee   daughter-in-law

> **Connect each English word to its correct translation:**

The sister-in-law •	La belle-fille
Me •	Le beau-fils
The daughter-in-law •	Le cousin
The cousin (fem.) •	La belle-mère
The in-laws •	Le beau-frère
The granddaughter •	La belle-soeur
The son-in-law •	La cousine
The cousin (masc.) •	Moi
The mother-in-law •	La belle-famille
The grandson •	Le beau-père
The brother-in-law •	Le petit-fils
The father-in-law •	La petite-fille

○ **Translate:** By memory only first, then fill in any missing words with help from the previous page.

The grandson	The daughter-in-law	The granddaughter
The cousin (masc.)	The father-in-law	The son-in-law
The sister-in-law	Me	The cousin (fem.)
The in-laws	The mother-in-law	The brother-in-law

Les relations - Relationships

Un couple

koopl   a couple

marrié/e

mah.ryeh   married

divorcé/e

dee.vor.seh   divorced

Célibataire

seh.lee.bah.tair   single

L'ex-femme

ex fahm   ex-wife

L'ex-mari

ex mah.ree   ex–husband

Veuf

vuhf   widower

Veuve

vuhv   widow

Un ami/Une amie

ah.mee   friend

La petit-amie

puh.tee.tah.mee   girlfriend

Le petit-ami

puh.tee.tah.mee   boyfriend

Le voisin/La voisine

vwah.zuh/vwah.zeen   neighbor

➤ Connect each English word to its correct translation:

Widow	L'ex-mari
Single	divorcé/e
The ex-husband	L'ex-femme
Divorced	La petite-amie
The girlfriend	Veuve
A friend	Célibataire
The neighbor	Un couple
Married	Le /La voisin(e)
The boyfriend	Veuf
The ex-wife	Un ami/Une amie
A couple	marrié(e)
Widower	Le petit-ami

Translate: By memory only first, then fill in any missing words with help from the previous page.

The boyfriend	Married	Divorced
Single	Widow	A friend (fem.)
Widower	Widow	The neighbor (masc.)
The ex-wife	The girlfriend	The ex-husband

Les emotions - Feelings (With Masc./Fem)

Heureux/Heureuse

uh.ruh / uh.ruhz   happy

Triste

treest   sad

en colère

ah koh.lair   angry

sérieux/sérieuse

sair.yuh / sair.yuhz serious

enthousiaste

ah.tooz.yahst   excited

effrayé(e)

eh.freh.yeh   afraid

curieux/curieuse

kür.yuh / kür.yuhz curious

anxieux/anxieuse

ahx.yuh /**ah**x.yuhz anxious

embarasassé(e)

ah.bah.rah.seh embarrassed

s'ennuyer

sah.nüee.yeh To be bored

supris/surprise

sür.pree/sür.preez surprised

concentré(e)

k**oh**.s**ah**.treh   focused

► **Connect each English word to its correct translation:**

Surprised •	Triste
Embarrassed •	En colère
Sad •	Effrayé/e
anxious •	Surpris/e
Serious •	Enthousiaste
Curious •	Embarassé/e
Happy •	Curieux/se *
Angry •	Sérieux/se *
Focused •	Concentré/e
To be bored •	Anxieux/se *
Excited •	Heureux/se *
Scared •	S'ennuyer

NOTE: I'm bored: **Je m'ennuie**   *Replace **x** by **se** with feminine subject.

➡ **Translate:** By memory only first, then fill in any missing words with help from the previous page.

Serious	Happy	To be bored
Sad	Anxious	Focused
Excited	Surprised	Embarrassed
Scared	Curious	Angry

Le corps humain - The human body

Le corps

kor   The body

La tête

tet   head

L'épaule
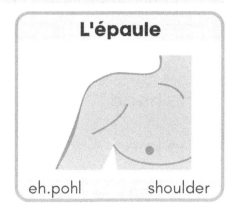
eh.pohl   shoulder

Le dos

doh   back

La poitrine

pwah.treen   chest

Le bras
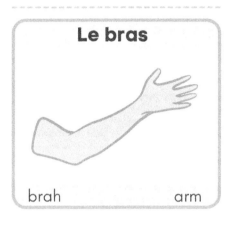
brah   arm

Le ventre
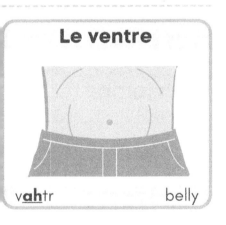
v**ah**tr   belly

La main
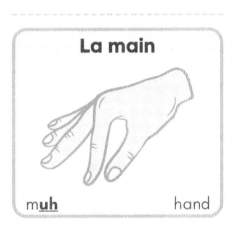
m**uh**   hand

Le doigt

dwah   finger

La jambe
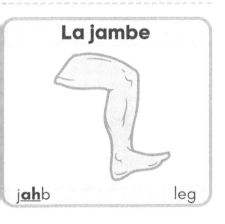
j**ah**b   leg

Le genou

juh.noo   knee

Le pied
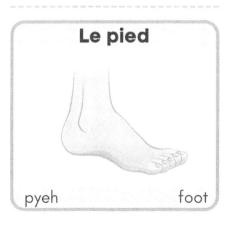
pyeh   foot

► **Connect each English word to its correct translation:**

The finger •	Le doigt
The head •	Le corps
The knee •	La poitrine
The arm •	Le ventre
The leg •	Le bras
The body •	La tête
The foot •	L'épaule
The chest •	La main
The shoulder •	Le dos
The hand •	Le genou
The back •	Le pied
The belly •	La jambe

Translate: By memory only first, then fill in any missing words with help from the previous page.

The belly	The arm	The knee
The foot	The chest	The back
The shoulder	The ankle	The leg
The hand	The head	The body

Le visage - The face

Le visage

vee.zahj   face

Le cou
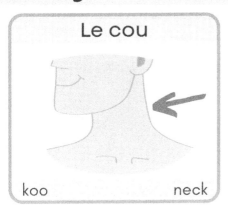
koo   neck

Les cheveux (m.)

shuh.vuh   hair

Le front
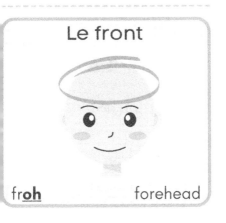
fr**oh**   forehead

Les yeux (m.)

leh zyuh   eyes

L'oreille (f.)

loh.rey   ear

Le nez
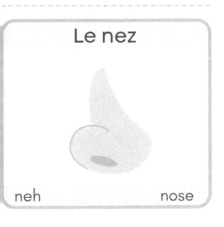
neh   nose

La joue

joo   cheek

La bouche

boosh   mouth

Les dents
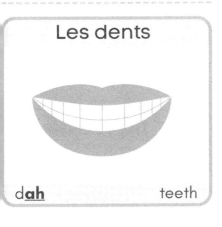
d**ah**   teeth

La langue

l**ah**g   tongue

Le menton

m**ah**.t**oh**   chin

► **Connect each English word to its correct translation:**

The hair •	Le front
The cheek •	Le cou
The nose •	Le menton
The forehead •	Le nez
The neck •	Les yeux
The teeth •	Le visage
The face •	La joue
The ear •	La bouche
The chin •	Les dents
The tongue •	La langue
The eyes •	Les cheveux
The mouth •	L'oreille

NOTE: The eye (singular): **L'oeil** (luh.yuh)

→ **Translate:** By memory only first, then fill in any missing words with help from the previous page.

The hair	The ear	The eye
_____	_____	_____
The nose	The neck	The chin
_____	_____	_____
The face	The teeth	The tongue
_____	_____	_____
The mouth	The forehead	The cheek
_____	_____	_____

Les organes - Organs

La peau

poh   skin

Les muscles (m.)
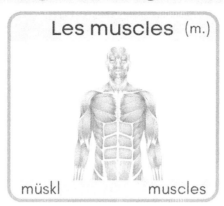
müskl   muscles

Les os (m.)
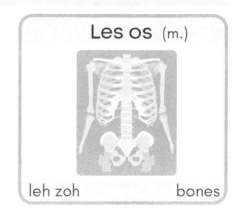
leh zoh   bones

Le cerveau
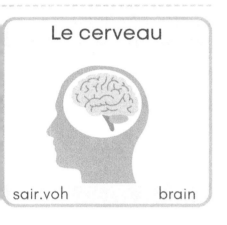
sair.voh   brain

Les poumons (m.)
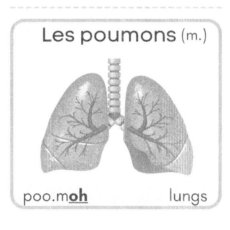
poo.**oh**   lungs

Le coeur

kuhr   heart

Les veines (f.)
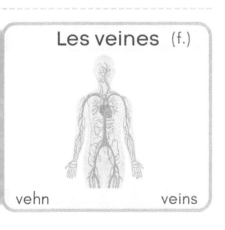
vehn   veins

Le foie
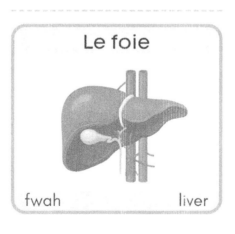
fwah   liver

L'estomac (m.)
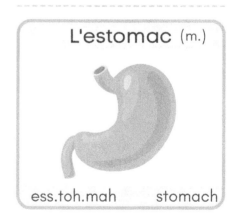
ess.toh.mah   stomach

L'intestin (m.)
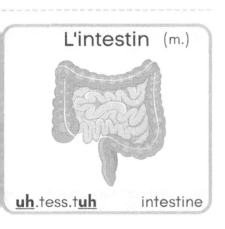
uh.tess.t**uh**   intestine

Les reins (m.)
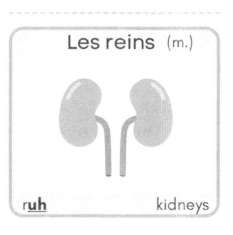
r**uh**   kidneys

La vessie
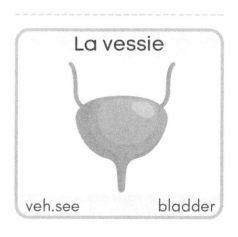
veh.see   bladder

▶ **Connect each English word to its correct translation:**

The heart •	Les os
The stomach •	Les poumons
The lungs •	La peau
The veins •	Les reins
The bones •	Les veines
The liver •	L'estomac
The skin •	La vessie
The kidneys •	Le foie
The muscles •	Le cerveau
The bladder •	Le coeur
The intestin •	L'intestin
The brain •	Les muscles

Translate: By memory only first, then fill in any missing words with help from the previous page.

The kidneys	The lungs	The bones
The muscles	The skin	The veins
The liver	The kidneys	The intestine
The heart	The bladder	The stomach

La maison - The house

La maison

may.z**oh**   house

Le toit

twah   roof

La porte

port   door

Le mur
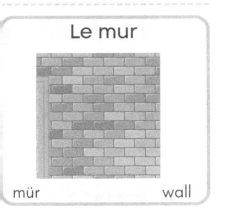
mür   wall

Le garage (m.)

gah.rahj   garage

Le jardin

jahr.d**uh**   backyard/garden

Le balcon

bahl.k**oh**   balcony

La cheminée

shuh.mee.neh   fireplace

La barrière

bahr.yair   fence

L'appartement (m.)

ah.pahr.tuh.m**ah**   apartment

L'étage (m.)
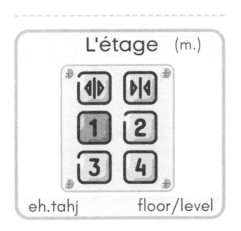
eh.tahj   floor/level

L'ascenseur (m.)
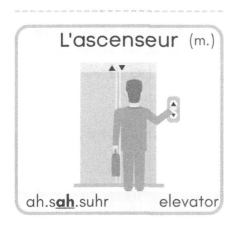
ah.s**ah**.suhr   elevator

> **Connect each English word to its correct translation:**

The wall	•	Le balcon
The fireplace	•	La barrière
The door	•	L'appartement
The fence	•	Le jardin
The house	•	La porte
The floor (level)	•	Le toit
The balcony	•	Le mur
The apartment	•	L'ascenseur
The backyard	•	La cheminée
The elevator	•	Le garage
The garage	•	La maison
The roof	•	L'étage

Translate: By memory only first, then fill in any missing words with help from the previous page.

The roof	The wall	The garage
The fence	The balcony	The elevator
The backyard	The house	The floor/level
The door	The fireplace	The apartment

Dans la maison - In the house

Le salon

sah.**loh**   living room

La cuisine

küee.zeen   kitchen

La salle à manger

sahl ah m**ah**.jeh dining room

La chambre

sh**ah**br   bedroom

La salle de bain

sahl duh b**uh**   bathroom

Les toilettes (f.)

twah.let   restrooms

La buanderie

bü.**ah**.dree   laundry room

Le sous-sol

soo sol   basement

Le grenier

gruh.nyeh   attic

Les escaliers

leh zess.kah.lyeh   stairs

Le couloir

kool.wahr   hallway

Le sol

sol   floor

The bedroom •	La salle de bain
The floor •	La buanderie
The stairs •	Le sous-sol
The basement •	La chambre
The laundry room •	Les escaliers
The bathroom •	Le salon
The living room •	Les toilettes
The attic •	Le sol
The hallway •	La cuisine
The restrooms •	Le grenier
The dining room •	Le couloir
The kitchen •	La salle a manger

⟳ **Translate:** By memory only first, then fill in any missing words with help from the previous page.

The stairs	The living room	The bedroom
_____	_____	_____
The bathroom	The attic	The restrooms
_____	_____	_____
The floor	The basement	The dining room
_____	_____	_____
The hallway	The kitchen	The laundry room
_____	_____	_____

Translate all the words your remember, check your answers with the word list in p.

1. The uncle •
2. The grandmother •
3. The niece •
4. The family •
5. The grandfather •
6. The nephew •
7. The father •
8. The aunt •
9. The daughter •
10. The son •
11. The brother •
12. The mother •
13. The sister •
14. The cousin (fem.) •
15. The grandson •
16. The brother-in-law •
17. The in-laws •
18. The son-in-law •
19. The cousin (masc.) •
20. The granddaughter •
21. The mother-in-law •
22. The father-in-law •
23. The daughter-in-law •
24. Me •
25. The sister-in-law •
26. Single •
27. Widow •

1. Divorced •
2. The ex-wife •
3. A couple •
4. The girlfriend •
5. The neighbor •
6. Married •
7. A friend •
8. The boyfriend •
9. Widower •
10. The ex-husband •
11. anxious •
12. To be bored •
13. Excited •
14. Serious •
15. Happy •
16. Angry •
17. Curious •
18. Focused •
19. Scared •
20. Sad •
21. Embarrassed •
22. Surprised •
23. The arm •
24. The leg •
25. The head •
26. The knee •
27. The finger •

Words to review:

Translate all the words your remember, check your answers with the word list in p.

1. The hand •	1. The bladder •
2. The back •	2. The intestin •
3. The foot •	3. The muscles •
4. The chest •	4. The brain •
5. The body •	5. The fence •
6. The shoulder •	6. The elevator •
7. The belly •	7. The garage •
8. The forehead •	8. The house •
9. The tongue •	9. The balcony •
10. The eyes •	10. The apartment •
11. The neck •	11. The floor (level) •
12. The face •	12. The backyard •
13. The ear •	13. The roof •
14. The teeth •	14. The door •
15. The chin •	15. The fireplace •
16. The mouth •	16. The wall •
17. The nose •	17. The basement •
18. The hair •	18. The restrooms •
19. The cheek •	19. The dining room •
20. The veins •	20. The laundry room •
21. The bones •	21. The living room •
22. The skin •	22. The attic •
23. The kidneys •	23. The bathroom •
24. The liver •	24. The hallway •
25. The lungs •	25. The kitchen •
26. The stomach •	26. The stairs •
27. The heart •	27. The floor (ground) •
	28. The bedroom •

<u>**Words to review:**</u>

La cuisine - The kitchen

Le réfrigérateur

reh.free.jeh.rah.tuhr fridge

Le placard

plah.kahr   cabinet

Le four

foor   oven

La cuisinière

kwee.zeen.yair   stove

Le comptoir

k**oh**.twahr   counter

L'évier   (m.)

lehv.yeh   sink

Le robinet

roh.bee.neh   faucet

Le micro-ondes

mee.kroh **oh**d   microwave

Le grille-pain

gree p**uh**   toaster

Le lave-vaisselle

lav vay.sel   dishwasher

La cafetière

kaft.yair   coffee machine

La poubelle

poo.bell trashcan/garbage

31

► **Connect each English word to its correct translation:**

The coffee machine	Le placard
The counter	Le réfrigérateur
The trash	La cafetière
The fridge	Le grille-pain
The sink	Le comptoir
The dishwasher	Le four
The cabinet	Le robinet
The toaster	La cuisinière
The oven	Le lave-vaisselle
The microwave	Le poubelle
The stove	L'évier
The faucet	Le micro-ondes

→ **Translate:** By memory only first, then fill in any missing words with help from the previous page.

The sink	The cabinet	The trash
The stove	The counter	The oven
The coffee machine	The faucet	The toaster
The dishwasher	The microwave	The fridge

Ustensils de cuisine - Kitchen tools

La casserole

kass.rol   saucepan

La poêle

pwahl   frying pan

La marmitte (m.)

mahr.meet   cooking pot

La spatule
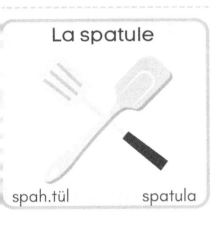
spah.tül   spatula

Le fouet

fway   whisk

Le torchon

tor.sh**oh**   (kitchen) towel

Le tablier

tah.blee.yeh   apron

La passoire

pass.wahr   colander

Le gant

g**ah**   oven mitt/glove

Le feu

fuh   fire

Le mixeur

mee.xuhr   blender

La théière

teh.yair   teapot

► **Connect each English word to its correct translation:**

The saucepan	•	Le torchon
The (kitchen) towel	•	Le tablier
The oven mitt	•	La marmite
The spatula	•	Le fouet
The fire	•	Le mixeur
The pot	•	La casserole
The colander	•	Le poêle
The teapot	•	Le gant
The blender	•	Le feu
The whisk	•	La théière
The apron	•	La spatule
The frying pan	•	La passoire

Translate: By memory only first, then fill in any missing words with help from the previous page.

The oven mitt/glove	The whisk	The teapot
The spatula	The saucepan	The colander
The pot	The apron	The blender
The frying pan	The fire	The (kitchen) towel

Le salon - The living room

Les meubles (m.)

muhbl   furniture

Le canapé

kah.nah.peh   couch

Le coussin

koo.su**h**   pillow

La télévision

teh.leh.vee.zy**oh**   television

La télécommande

teh.leh.koh.m**ah**d   remote control

La table basse

tabl bass   coffee table

L'horloge (f.)

or.loj   clock

La photo

foh.toh   picture

La lumière

lüm.yair   light

Le tableau

tah.bloh   painting

Le tapis

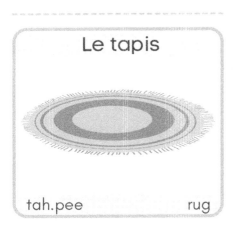

tah.pee   rug

Les rideaux

ree.doh   curtains

► **Connect each English word to its correct translation:**

The picture •	La table basse
The curtains •	La télécommande
The coffee table •	Le canapé
The television •	La photo
The rug •	L'horloge
The remote control •	Le tableau
The clock •	Les rideaux
The couch •	La télévision
The furniture •	Le tapis
The light •	La lumière
The pillow •	Le coussin
The painting •	Les meubles

Translate: By memory only first, then fill in any missing words with help from the previous page.

The coffee table	The couch	The television
The remote	The painting	The picture
The rug	The furniture	The clock
The pillow	The curtains	The light

La salle à manger - The dining room

La table

tahbl   table

L'assiette (f.)

ahss.yet   plate

La serviette

sairv.yet   napkin

La fourchette

foor•shet   fork

La cuillère

küee.yair   spoon

Le couteau

koo.toh   knife

Le verre

vair   glass/cup

La bouteille

boo.tey   bottle

Le plateau

plah.toh   tray

Le repas

ruh.pah   meal

La nappe

nap   tablecloth

Le vase

vahz   vase

► **Connect each English word to its correct translation:**

The napkin •	La fourchette
The table •	Le vase
The knife •	L'assiette
The spoon •	La bouteille
The bottle •	La serviette
The meal •	Le verre
The fork •	La cuillère
The vase •	La nappe
The plate •	Le plateau
The cup/glass •	La table
The tablecoth •	La fourchette
The tray •	Le repas

○ **Translate:** By memory only first, then fill in any missing words with help from the previous page.

The knife	The cup/glass	The spoon
The plate	The napkin	The tablecloth
The table	The tray	The bottle
The vase	The meal	The fork

La chambre - The bedroom

La fenêtre

fuh•naytr   window

Le lit

lee   bed

Le matelas

mat.lah   mattress

L'oreiller (m.)

oh.reh.yeh   pillow (for bed)

Le drap

drah   sheet

La couverture

koo.vair.tür   blanket

La table de nuit

tahbl duh nüee   nightstand

Le réveil

reh.vey   alarm clock

L'armoire

arm.wahr   closet

Le bureau

bü.roh   desk

La chaise

shayz   chair

La lampe

lahp   lamp

► Connect each English word to its correct translation:

The closet	•	Le bureau
The chair	•	Le drap
The nightstand	•	La chaise
The sheet	•	La lampe
The mattress	•	La couverture
The window	•	Le réveil
The desk	•	Le lit
The alarm clock	•	Le matelas
The blanket	•	L'oreiller
The bed	•	La fenêtre
The pillow	•	La table de nuit
The lamp	•	Le placard

Translate: By memory only first, then fill in any missing words with help from the previous page.

The desk	The lamp	The closet
The pillow	The bed	The window
The chair	The alarm clock	The mattress
The sheet	The nightstand	The blanket

La salle de bain - The bathroom

La douche

doosh   shower

La baignoire

bayn.wahr   bathtub

La serviette

sairv.yet   towel

Le shampoing

sh**ah**.pw**uh**   shampoo

L'après-shampoing
(m.)

ah.pray
sh**ah**.pw**uh**   conditioner

Le savon

sah.v**oh**   soap

La brosse
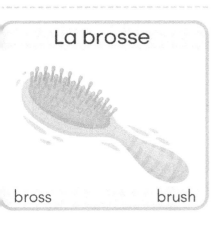
bross   brush

La brosse à dents

bross ah d**ah**   toothbrush

Le dentifrice
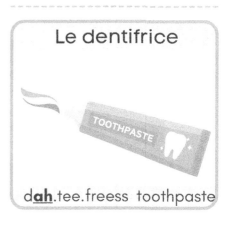
d**ah**.tee.freess   toothpaste

Le rasoir

rahz.wahr   razor

Le miroir

meer.wahr   mirror

Le papier toilette

pa.pyeh twah.let   toilet paper

▶ **Connect each English word to its correct translation:**

The toothpaste	•	Le rasoir
The brush	•	La boignoire
The soap	•	La serviette
The mirror	•	L'après-shampoing
The shower	•	Le dentifrice
The shampoo	•	Le miroir
The toothbrush	•	Le papier toilette
The bathtub	•	Le savon
The razor	•	Le shampoing
The towel	•	Le douche
The conditioner	•	La brosse
The toilet paper	•	La brosse à dents

→ **Translate:** By memory only first, then fill in any missing words with help from the previous page.

The brush	The toothbrush	The conditioner
The mirror	The soap	The towel
The shampoo	The toothpaste	The razor
The toilet paper	The bathtub	The shower

La buanderie - The laundry room

La machine à laver

mah.sheen ah lah.veh   washer

Le sèche-linge

saysh l**uh**j   dryer

La lessive

leh.seev   laundry/ laundry soap

Le linge sale

l**uh**j sahl   dirty clothes

Le panier à linge

pah.nyeh ah l**uh**j   laundry basket

L'adoucissant

lah.doo.see.s**ah**   fabric softener

L'aspirateur (m.)
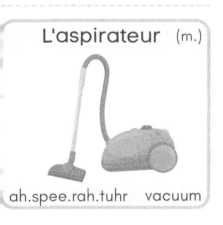
ah.spee.rah.tuhr   vacuum

Le balai

bah.lay   broom

La pelle

pel   dust pan

La serpillère

sair.pee.yair   mop

Le sceau

soh   bucket

Le fer à repasser

fair ah ruh.pah.seh   iron

► **Connect each English word to its correct translation:**

The mop •	La lessive
The laundry basket •	Le sceau
The vacuum •	L'adoucissant
The laundry soap/ The laundry •	La machine à laver
The bucket •	Le fer à repasser
The washer •	Le panier à linge
The dust pan •	La serpillère
The dryer •	Le balai
The iron •	Le linge sale
The dirty clothes •	L'aspirateur
The broom •	Le sèche-linge
The fabric softener •	La pelle

➡ **Translate:** By memory only first, then fill in any missing words with help from the previous page.

The bucket	The dirty clothes	The dust pan
The broom	The mop	The vacuum
The iron	The laundry basket	The fabric softener
The dryer	The laundry soap/laundry	The washer

Les vêtements - The clothes

Les vêtements

vay.tuh.m**ah**   clothes

Le manteau

m**ah**.toh   coat

La veste

vest   jacket

Le pull

pül   sweater

Le tshirt

tee.shurt   t-shirt

La chemise

shuh.meez   shirt

Le pantalon

p**ah**.t**ah**.l**oh**   pants

La robe

rob   dress

La jupe

jüp   skirt

Le short

short   short

Le costume

kohs.tüm   suit

Les chaussettes

shoh.set   socks

Connect each English word to its correct translation:

The short   •   Le costume

The dress   •   La jupe

The shirt   •   Le pantalon

The sweater   •   Le short

The coat   •   Les chaussettes

The socks   •   Le pull

The pants   •   Les vêtements

The t-shirt   •   La veste

The skirt   •   La chemise

The clothes   •   Le manteau

The jacket   •   La robe

The suit   •   Le tshirt

Translate: By memory only first, then fill in any missing words with help from the previous page.

The skirt	The socks	The dress
The t-shirt	The pants	The suit
The short	The sweater	The shirt
The clothes	The jacket	The coat

Les accessoires - The accessories

Le caleçon

kahl.**soh**   boxer short

La culotte

kü.lot   panties

Le soutien-gorge

soo.ty**uh** gorj   bra

Les chaussures

shoh.sür   shoes

Le chapeau

shah.poh   hat

Le sac à main

sak ah m**uh**   purse

La ceinture

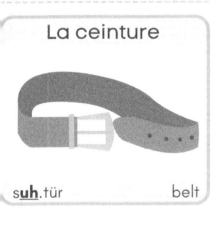

s**uh**.tür   belt

La cravate

krah.vat   tie

L'écharpe (f.)

eh.sharp   scarf

Le collier

koh.lyeh   necklace

Les boucles d'oreilles

bookl doh.rey   earings

La bague

bag   ring

The necklace •	Le sac à main
The purse •	Le collier
The panties •	Le soutien-gorge
The bra •	La bague
The shoes •	La cravate
The scarf •	La culotte
The hat •	Les chaussures
The belt •	La ceinture
The earrings •	Le caleçon
The tie •	Le chapeau
The boxer short •	L'écharpe
The ring •	Les boucles d'oreilles

Translate: By memory only first, then fill in any missing words with help from the previous page.

The necklace	The belt	The earings
The boxer short	The ring	The panties
The tie	The scarf	The bra
The shoes	The purse	The hat

Translate all the words your remember, check your answers with the word list in p.

1. The fridge •	1. The television •
2. The microwave •	2. The light •
3. The stove •	3. The pillow •
4. The sink •	4. The rug •
5. The cabinet •	5. The clock •
6. The toaster •	6. The couch •
7. The dishwasher •	7. The remote control •
8. The oven •	8. The furniture •
9. The faucet •	9. The painting •
10. The trash •	10. The spoon •
11. The counter •	11. The cup/glass •
12. The spatula •	12. The tablecoth •
13. The whisk •	13. The bottle •
14. The apron •	14. The fork •
15. The fire •	15. The vase •
16. The colander •	16. The meal •
17. The teapot •	17. The plate •
18. The pot •	18. The tray •
19. The blender •	19. The knife •
20. The frying pan •	20. The table •
21. The oven mitt •	21. The napkin •
22. The kitchen towel •	22. The sheet •
23. The saucepan •	23. The mattress •
24. The coffee table •	24. The window •
25. The curtains •	25. The nightstand •
26. The picture •	26. The chair •
27. The coffee machine •	27. The closet •

Words to review:

Translate all the words your remember, check your answers with the word list in p.

1. The bed	•	
2. The pillow	•	
3. The desk	•	
4. The alarm clock	•	
5. The blanket	•	
6. The lamp	•	
7. The mirror	•	
8. The towel	•	
9. The conditioner	•	
10. The shower	•	
11. The toothbrush	•	
12. The bathtub	•	
13. The shampoo	•	
14. The razor	•	
15. The toilet paper	•	
16. The soap	•	
17. The brush	•	
18. The toothpaste	•	
19. The dirty clothes	•	
20. The broom	•	
21. The bucket	•	
22. The dust pan	•	
23. The iron	•	
24. The fabric softener	•	
25. The laundry basket	•	
26. The laundry/	•	
The laundry soap	•	

1. The dryer •
2. The washer •
3. The vacuum •
4. The mop •
5. The sweater •
6. The clothes •
7. The jacket •
8. The coat •
9. The pants •
10. The t-shirt •
11. The tuxedo •
12. The skirt •
13. The suit •
14. The shirt •
15. The dress •
16. The short •
17. The bra •
18. The tie •
19. The boxer short •
20. The shoes •
21. The hat •
22. The belt •
23. The scarf •
24. The earrings •
25. The ring •
26. The panties •
27. The purse •
28. The necklace •

Words to review:

Dans le sac à main - In the purse

Le porte-feuille

port fuh.yuh   wallet

Les cléfs (f.)

kleh   keys

L'argent (m.)

ahr.j**ah**   money

La monnaie

moh.nay   change

La carte de crédit

kart duh kreh.dee   credit card

La carte d'identité

kart dee.d**ah**.tee.teh   I.D card

Le permis de conduire

pair.mee duh k**oh**.düeer   driver's licence

La montre
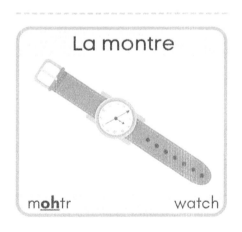
m**oh**tr   watch

Le parapluie

pah.rah.plüee   umbrella

Le maquillage

mah.kee.yaj   makeup

Le mouchoir

moosh.war   tissue

Le rouge à lèvres

rooj ah layvr   lipstick

Connect each English word to its correct translation:

The credit card	•	Le maquillage
The keys	•	Le permis de conduire
The I.D card	•	Le parapluie
The umbrella	•	Le porte-feuilles
The change	•	La monnaie
The driver's license	•	Le rouge à lèvres
The makeup	•	La carte d'identité
The lipstick	•	La montre
The money	•	Le mouchoir
The wallet	•	L'argent
The tissue	•	La carte de crédit
The watch	•	Les clefs

Translate: By memory only first, then fill in any missing words with help from the previous page.

The umbrella	The watch	The keys
The lipstick	The credit card	The tissue
The driver's license	I.D card	The change
The wallet	The money	The makeup

La technologie - The technology

Le téléphone portable

teh.leh.fon por.tahbl — cell phone

Le téléphone

teh.leh.fon — phone

L'ordinateur portable (m.)

or.dee.nah.tuhr por.tahbl — laptop

La souris

soo.ree — mouse

Le clavier

klah.vyeh — keyboard

L'écran (m.)
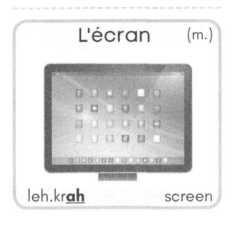
leh.kr**ah** — screen

Le wifi

wee.fee — wifi

Le modem

moh.dem — modem

La prise

preez — plug

Le chargeur

shar.juhr — charger

Connecté

koh.nek.teh — connected

Pas de réseau

pah duh reh.zoh — no service

Connect each English word to its correct translation:

The mouse •	Le téléphone
The keyboard •	L'ordinateur portable
The laptop •	connecté
The wifi •	La souris
The plug •	L'écran
The phone •	Le téléphone portable
The screen •	Le modem
The cell phone •	La prise
The no service •	Le wifi
The charger •	Le clavier
The connected •	Pas de réseau
The modem •	Le chargeur

Translate: By memory only first, then fill in any missing words with help from the previous page.

The keyboard	connected	The screen
___	___	___
wifi	The phone	modem
___	___	___
The cell phone	No service	The laptop
___	___	___
The plug	The mouse	The chargeur
___	___	___

Les jours - The days

Lundi

luhn.dee   Monday

Mardi

mahr.dee   Tuesday

Mercredi

mair.kruh.dee   Wednesday

jeudi

juh.dee   Thursday

vendredi

vah.druh.dee   Friday

samedi

sam.dee   Saturday

dimanche

dee.mahsh   Sunday

Weekend

week.end   weekend

Le jour

joor   day

La semaine

suh.men   week

Le mois

mwah   month

L'année

ah.neh   year

> **Connect each English word to its correct translation:**

The week •	Le jour
Wednesday •	mercredi
The month •	mardi
Tuesday •	weekend
Friday •	dimanche
Thursday •	lundi
The year •	samedi
Monday •	Le mois
The weekend •	L'année
Sunday •	vendredi
The day •	La semaine
Saturday •	jeudi

Days of the week are not capitalized in French.

Translate: By memory only first, then fill in any missing words with help from the previous page.

The weekend	The year	Tuesday
Monday	Wednesday	Friday
Sunday	The week	Saturday
The day	Thursday	The month

Le temps - Time

Aujourd'hui

oh.joor.düee today

Demain
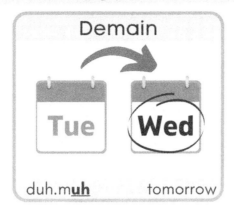
duh.m**uh** tomorrow

Hier

ee.yair yesterday

Avant-hier
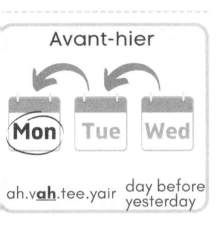
ah.v**ah**.tee.yair day before yesterday

La semaine dernière

suh.men dair.nyair last week

La semaine prochaine
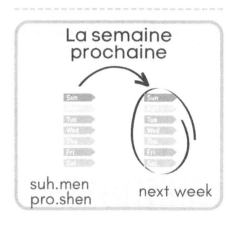
suh.men pro.shen next week

Le mois dernier

mwah dair.nyeh last month

Le mois prochain
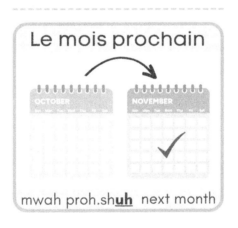
mwah proh.sh**uh** next month

L'année dernière

ah.neh dair.nyair last year

L'année prochaine

ah.neh proh.shen next year

il y a deux ans

eel.ee.yah duh z**ah** 2 years ago

Dans deux ans

d**ah** duh z**ah** In 2 years

► **Connect each English word to its correct translation:**

Last month •	Avant-hier
Tomorrow •	Le mois prochain
Next week •	Il y a deux ans
Today •	Aujourd'hui
Last year •	La semaine dernière
2 years ago •	Dans deux ans
Yesterday •	L'année prochaine
Next month •	Le mois dernier
In 2 years •	L'année dernière
The day before yesterday •	La semaine prochaine
Last week •	Demain
Last year •	Hier

→ **Translate:** By memory only first, then fill in any missing words with help from the previous page.

Last week	Yesterday	Last year
The day before yesterday	2 years ago	Today
Next month	Next week	Last month
Tomorrow	Next year	In 2 years

La journée - The day/daytime

Le jour

joor   day

La nuit

nüee   night

Le matin

mah.t**uh**   morning

L'après-midi (m.)

ah.pray mee.dee afternoon

Le soir

swahr   night

Midi

mee.dee   noon

Minuit

mee.nüee   midnight

Le lever du soleil

luh.veh dü soh.ley   sunrise

Le coucher du soleil

koo.sheh dü soh.ley   sunset

La seconde

suh.g**oh**nd   second

La minute

mee.nüt   minute

L'heure

uhr   hour

59

► Connect each English word to its correct translation:

The minute •	La nuit
The sunrise •	Minuit
The second •	Le coucher du soleil
The night •	L'après-midi
The morning •	Le matin
Noon •	Le soir
The afternoon •	Le jour
The sunset •	L'heure
The hour •	La minute
The evening •	La seconde
Midnight •	Midi
The day •	Le lever du soleil

Translate: By memory only first, then fill in any missing words with help from the previous page.

The morning	Midnight	The hour
The second	The day	Noon
The evening	The night	The sunrise
The afternoon	The minute	The sunset

Les mois - The months

janvier

jahv.yeh   January

février

feh.vree.yeh   February

mars

mahrs   March

avril

ah.vreel   April

mai

may   May

juin

jwuh   June

juillet

jwee.yeh   July

août

oot   August

septembre

sep.tahbr   September

octobre

ohk.tobr   October

novembre

noh.vahbr   November

décembre

deh.sahbr   December

Connect each English word to its correct translation:

February •	mars
June •	janvier
March •	juillet
December •	juin
September •	décembre
May •	mai
August •	octobre
January •	février
November •	avril
October •	septembre
July •	août
April •	novembre

Months are not capitalized in French.

Translate: By memory only first, then fill in any missing words with help from the previous page.

January	April	May
December	August	February
Septembre	March	November
June	October	July

Le temps/ les saisons - Time / Seasons

Le soleil  soh.ley sun	**La pluie**  plwee rain	**Le nuage**  nü.ahj cloud
Le vent 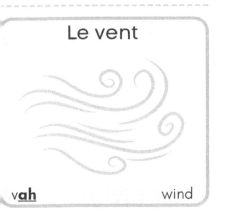 v**ah** wind	**La neige**  nayj snow	**L'ouragan** (m.)  oo.rah.**gah** hurricane
La tempête  t**ah**.pet storm	**La saison**  seh.z**oh** season	**Le printemps**  pr**uh**•t**ah** spring
L'été (m.)  eh.teh summer	**L'automne** (m.)  oh.ton fall	**L'hiver** (m.)  ee.vair winter

► **Connect each English word to its correct translation:**

The cloud	•	Le vent
The spring	•	La tempête
The sun	•	L'été
The season	•	Le nuage
The wind	•	Le printemps
The storm	•	La neige
The fall	•	Le soleil
The rain	•	L'hiver
The summer	•	La pluie
The hurricane	•	La saison
The winter	•	L'ouragan
The snow	•	L'automne

⟳ **Translate:** By memory only first, then fill in any missing words with help from the previous page.

The rain	The season	The wind
The snow	The winter	The hurricane
The storm	The fall	The sun
The summer	The cloud	The spring

Les étapes de la vie - Life milestones

La naissance

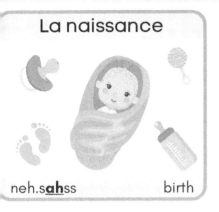

neh.**sah**ss   birth

L'anniversaire (m.)

ah.nee.vair.sair   birthday

La rentrée

r**ah**.treh   1st day of school

Obtenir un diplôme

ob.tuh.neer **uh** dee.plohm   get a degree

Obtenir un emploi

ob.tuh.neer **uh** n**ah**.plwah   get a job

Voyager

vwah.yah.jeh   travel

Tomber amoureux

t**oh**.beh ah.moo.ruh   fall in love

Se marrier

suh mah.ryeh   get married

Tomber enceinte

t**oh**.beh **ah**.s**uh**t   get pregnant

Élever des enfants

eh.luh.veh deh z**ah**.f**ah**   raise children

La retraite

ruh.tret   retirement

La mort

mohr   death

► **Connect each English word to its correct translation:**

The birthday •	Se marrier
Get a job •	La rentrée
(The) birth •	La retraite
Get married •	L'anniversaire
1st day of school •	Obtenir un diplôme
Retirement •	La naissance
Get a degree •	Voyager
(The) death •	Tomber enceinte
To get pregnant •	La mort
To travel •	Tomber * amoureux
Raise children •	Obtenir un emploi
To fall in love •	Élever des enfants

* amoureu**x** = for a man   amoureu**se** = for a woman

→ **Translate:** By memory only first, then fill in any missing words with help from the previous page.

Get a job	The 1st day of school	(To) Get pregnant
The retirement	Get a degree	(The) birth
(The) death	To fall in love	(To) raise children
To travel	(To) Get married	The birthday

La fête - The party

La fête

fet   party

Joyeux anniversaire

jwah.yuh   Happy
zah.nee.vair.sair   birthday

Le marriage (m.)

mahr.yahj   wedding

Félicitations!

feh.lee.see.
tah.sy**oh**   congratulations

Les invités

leh z**uh**.vee.teh   guests

Le gâteau d'anniversaire

gah.toh   birthday
dah.nee.vair.sair   cake

La bougie

boo.jee   candle

Les décorations (f.)

deh.koh.rah.sy**oh**   decorations

Le cadeau

kah.doh   gift

Les ballons (m.)

bah.l**oh**   balloons

Le bouquet de fleurs

boo.keh duh fluhr   flower
                 bouquet

Les feux d'artifice (m.)

fuh dahr.tee.fees   fireworks

► **Connect each English word to its correct translation:**

The balloons •   Le gâteau d'anniversaire

The candle •   Félicitations!

The decorations •   Les ballons

The fireworks •   Le cadeau

The party •   Le bouquet de fleurs

Happy birthday! •   Joyeux anniversaire!

The birthday cake •   Les invités

The guests •   Le marriage

Congratulations! •   La fête

The gift •   Les décorations

The wedding •   La bougie

The flower bouquet •   Les feux d'artifice

⊙ **Translate:** By memory only first, then fill in any missing words with help from the previous page.

The flower bouquet	The guests	The gift
The birthday cake	The fireworks	The party
The balloons	The decorations	The wedding
Congratulations!	The candle	Happy birthday!

Translate all the words your remember, check your answers with the word list in p.

1. The umbrella	•	1. Tuesday	•
2. The wallet	•	2. Sunday	•
3. The tissue	•	3. The day	•
4. The change	•	4. Friday	•
5. The makeup	•	5. The year	•
6. The lipstick	•	6. Monday	•
7. The money	•	7. Thursday	•
8. The watch	•	8. The weekend	•
9. The I.D card	•	9. Saturday	•
10. The keys	•	10. Today	•
11. The credit card	•	11. Last week	•
12. The wifi	•	12. Last year	•
13. The charger	•	13. Yesterday	•
14. The connected	•	14. Next month	•
15. The plug	•	15. 2 years ago	•
16. The screen	•	16. In 2 years	•
17. The cell phone	•	17. Last year	•
18. The phone	•	18. Next week	•
19. The no service	•	19. Tomorrow	•
20. The modem	•	20. Last month	•
21. The laptop	•	21. The night	•
22. The keyboard	•	22. The morning	•
23. The mouse	•	23. Noon	•
24. The month	•	24. The second	•
25. Wednesday	•	25. The sunrise	•
26. The week	•	26. The minute	•
27. The driver's license	•	27. The day before yesterday	•

Words to review:

Translate all the words your remember, check your answers with the word list in p.

A	B
1. The evening •	1. The hurricane •
2. Midnight •	2. The winter •
3. The afternoon •	3. The snow •
4. The sunset •	4. Get married •
5. The hour •	5. To travel •
6. The day •	6. Raise children •
7. December •	7. 1st day of school •
8. October •	8. Get a degree •
9. July •	9. (The) death •
10. September •	10. Retirement •
11. August •	11. To get pregnant •
12. January •	12. To fall in love •
13. May •	13. (The) birth •
14. November •	14. Get a job •
15. April •	15. The birthday •
16. March •	16. The fireworks •
17. June •	17. The gift •
18. February •	18. The wedding •
19. The season •	19. The party •
20. The wind •	20. The birthday cake •
21. The fall •	21. The guests •
22. The rain •	22. Happy birthday! •
23. The storm •	23. Congratulations! •
24. The summer •	24. The flower bouquet •
25. The sun •	25. The decorations •
26. The spring •	26. The candle •
27. The cloud •	27. The balloons •

Words to review:

Les jours de fêtes - The holidays/special days

Le Nouvel An

noo.vel **ah**   New Year

Réveillon du Nouvel An

reh.veh.y**oh** dü noo.vel **ah**   New Year's Eve

Bonne Année!

bonah.neh Happy New Year!

Noël

noh.el   Christmas

Réveillon de Noël

reh.veh.y**oh** duh noh.el   Christmas Eve

Joyeux Noël

jwah.yuh noh.el   Merry Christmas

Le jour férié

joor fair.yeh   public holiday

Pâques

pahk   Easter

La Fête des Mères

fet deh mair   Mother's Day

Bonne Fête * des Mères

bon fet deh mair   Happy Mother's Day

La Fête des Pères

fet deh pair   Father's Day

Bonne Fête * des Pères

bon fet deh pair   Happy Father's Day

► **Connect each English word to its correct translation:**

Happy New Year •	Le Réveillon de Noël
Easter •	La fête des Pères
Mother's Day •	Le Réveillon du Nouvel an
New Year's day •	Joyeux Noël
Christmas Eve •	Bonne année!
Public holiday •	Pâques
New Year's Eve •	Le Nouvel an
Merry Christmas •	Bonne Fête* des Pères
Happy Mother's Day •	Noël
Father's Day •	La fête des Mères
Happy Father's Day •	Bonne Fête* des Mères
Christmas •	Jour férié

*__Bonne__ may be replaced by __Joyeuse__: "Joyeuse fête des mères/pères"

→ **Translate:** By memory only first, then fill in any missing words with help from the previous page.

Happy Mother's Day	Easter	New Year's Eve
_____	_____	_____
Merry Christmas	New Year's Day	Happy Father's Day
_____	_____	_____
Father's Day	Public holiday	Christmas
_____	_____	_____
Happy New Year!	Christmas Eve	Mother's Day
_____	_____	_____

Les cadeaux - The gifts

Le jouet

joo.eh   toy

La console de jeu

k**oh**.sol duh juh   gaming console

Le jeu video

juh vee.deh.oh   video game

Le vélo

veh.loh   bicycle

Le jeu de société

juh duh soh.syeh.teh   board game

La balle / Le ballon

bahl / bah.**loh**   ball

L'instrument (m.)
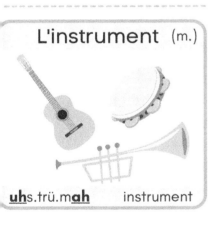
uhs.trü.m**ah**   instrument

La poupée

poo.peh   doll

Le robot

roh.boh   robot

La peluche

puh.lüsh   stuffed toy

Les bijoux (m.)

bee.joo   jewelry

La carte-cadeau

kart kah.doh   gift card

Connect each English word to its correct translation:

The jewelry •	La carte-cadeau
The toy •	Le robot
The gaming console •	Le jouet
The ball •	La peluche
The instrument •	Le jeu vidéo
The stuffed animal •	Le vélo
The board game •	Les bijoux
The robot •	Le jeu de société
The bicycle •	La balle/Le ballon
The gift card •	La console de jeu
The video game •	L'instrument
The doll •	La poupée

Translate: By memory only first, then fill in any missing words with help from the previous page.

The ball	The video game	The stuffed animal
_____	_____	_____
The gift card	The doll	The bicycle
_____	_____	_____
The toy	The board game	The jewelry
_____	_____	_____
The instrument	The gaming console	The robot
_____	_____	_____

L'école - The school

La crèche

kresh — nursery

La maternelle

mah.tair.nel — preschool

L'école primaire (f.)

eh.kol pree.mair — elemetary school

Le collège

koh.layj — middle school

Le lycée

lee.seh — high school

L'université

ü.nee.vair.see.teh — university

L'élève

eh.lev — young student

L'étudiant (m.)

eh.tüd.**yah** — older student

L'examen

eh.xah.m**uh** — exam

Les notes (f.)
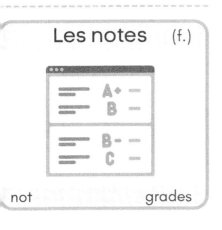
not — grades

Les devoirs (m.)

duh.vwahr — homework

La leçon

luh.s**oh** — lesson

▶ Connect each English word to its correct translation:

The middle school •	Le lycée
The student (child) •	L'université
The high school •	La crèche
The preschool •	L'étudiant
The homework •	Le collège
The elemetary school •	Les notes
The older student (teen & up) •	La maternelle
The exam •	L'élève
The nursery •	Les devoirs
The lesson •	L'école primaire
The university •	La leçon
The grades •	L'examen

⚠ étudiant: male student ➡ étudiante: female student

Translate: By memory only first, then fill in any missing words with help from the previous page.

The student (teen & up)	The middle school	The homework
The exam	The nursery	The lesson
The elemetary school	The university	The preschool
The student (child)	The grades	The high school

Dans la classe - In the classroom

La classe

klass   classroom

Le professeur

proh.feh.suhr   teacher

Le livre

leevr   book

Le cahier

kah.yeh   notebook

La feuille de papier

fuh.yuh duh pap.yeh   sheet of paper

Le stylo
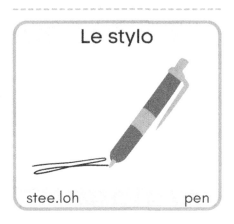
stee.loh   pen

Le crayon

kreh.y**oh**   pencil

Les ciseaux

see.zoh   scissors

La colle

kol   glue

La gomme

gom   eraser

La calculatrice

kahl.kü.lah.trees   calculator

Le tableau
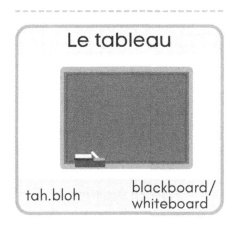
tah.bloh   blackboard/whiteboard

The book	•	La feuille de papier
The scissors	•	La gomme
The pen	•	Le livre
The blackboard/ whiteboard	•	La classe
The classroom	•	Le stylo
The notebook	•	Le cahier
The calculator	•	Les ciseaux
The eraser	•	Le professeur
The teacher	•	La calculatrice
The glue	•	Le crayon
The pencil	•	Le tableau
The sheet of paper	•	La colle

Translate: By memory only first, then fill in any missing words with help from the previous page.

The pencil	The scissors	The book
___	___	___
The teacher	The pen	The eraser
___	___	___
The sheet of paper	The classroom	The notebook
___	___	___
The calculator	The glue	The blackboard/ whiteboard
___	___	___

Les matières - The subjects

La langue étrangère

lahg eh.tr**ah**.jair   foreign language

Les maths
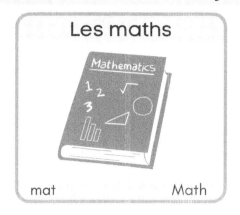
mat   Math

L'algèbre
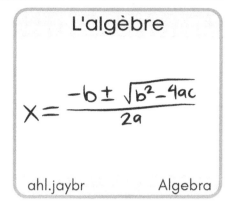

$$x = \frac{-b \pm \sqrt{b^2 - 4ac}}{2a}$$

ahl.jaybr   Algebra

La géométrie
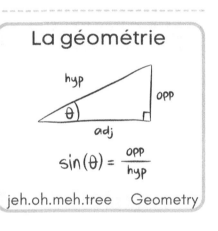

$$\sin(\theta) = \frac{opp}{hyp}$$

jeh.oh.meh.tree   Geometry

L'histoire

eess.twahr   History

La géographie

jeh.oh.grah.fee   Geography

La chimie
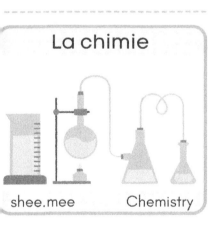
shee.mee   Chemistry

La biologie
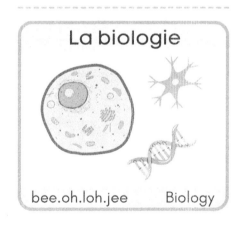
bee.oh.loh.jee   Biology

La physique
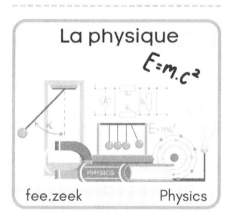

$E = m.c^2$

fee.zeek   Physics

La littérature

lee.teh.rah.tür   Literature

La science

see.**ah**ss   Science

L'art

ahr   Art

▶ Connect each English word to its correct translation:

The foreign language •	La littérature
Science •	La langue étrangère
Algebra •	La physique
Geography •	L'algèbre
Math •	Les maths
Chemistry •	La chimie
Physics •	La géométrie
Geometry •	L'art
Literature •	L'histoire
Biology •	La science
Art •	La biologie
History •	La géographie

Translate: By memory only first, then fill in any missing words with help from the previous page.

Chemistry	Physics	Biology
Literature	The foreign language	Algebra
Geometry	Art	Geography
Science	History	Math

Les professions - The professions

Le gérant (manager)

jeh.**rah**   manager

L'employé

ah.plwah.yeh   employee

Le dentiste

d**ah**.teest   dentist

L'ingénieur

uh.jehn.yuhr   engineer

Le comptable

k**oh**.tahbl   accountant

L'avocat

ah.voh.kah   lawyer

Le médecin/docteur

med.s**uh**   doctor

L'infirmier

uh.feerm.yeh   nurse

L'artiste

ahr.teest   artist

Le pompier

p**oh**p.yeh   fireman

Le policier

poh.lees.yeh   policeman

L'homme d'affaires

om dah.fair   businessman

▶ **Connect each English word to its correct translation :** *(female version)*

The business woman •	La pompière
The nurse •	L'avocate
The woman firefighter •	La gérante/ La manager
The lawyer •	L'infirmière
The manager •	La dentiste
The engineer •	L'employée
The policewoman •	Le médecin
The doctor •	L'ingénieure
The dentist •	L'artiste
The employee •	La femme d'affaire
The accountant •	La policière
The artist •	La comptable

- **" Le" médecin** can be used for both men and women.
- **médecin**: general doctor. **Docteur**: usually, specialist.

Translate: By memory only first, then fill in any missing words with help from the previous page. *(write the version indicated in parenthesis)*

The nurse (f.)	The firefighter (m.)	The artist (m)
The policewoman	The engineer (m.)	The doctor (m.)
The lawyer (f.)	The dentist (f.)	The businessman
The employee (f.)	The accountant (f.)	The manager (m.)

Au travail - At work

Le directeur

dee.rek.tuhr   director/CEO

Le/La secretaire

suh.kreh.tair   secretary

Le collègue

koh.leg   colleague

L'ordinateur (m.)
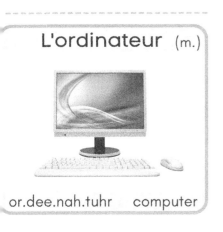
or.dee.nah.tuhr   computer

L'imprimante (f.)

uh.pree.m**ah**t   printer

La réunion

reh.ün.y**oh**   meeting

L'entretien

ah.trut.y**uh**   interview

Le chômage

shoh.mahj   unemployement

Être embauché

aytr **ah**.boh.sheh to be hired

Être licencié

aytr lee.s**ah**.syeh to be fired

Le salaire

sah.lair   salary

Être à la retraite

aytr ah la ruh.tret to be retired

Connect each English word to its correct translation:

The colleague	L'ordinateur
To be retired	Le directeur
The computer	Le salaire
The director/CEO	L'imprimante
The interview	Être embauché
To be hired	Être licencié
The secretary	Le/La secretaire
The unemployement	L'entretien
To be fired	La réunion
The meeting	Le collègue
The salary	Être à la retraite
The printer	Le chômage

Translate: By memory only first, then fill in any missing words with help from the previous page.

To be retired	The secretary	To be hired
The director/CEO	To be fired	The printer
The unemployement	The colleague	The interview
The computer	The meeting	The salary

La ville - The city

La ville
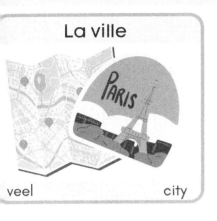
veel   city

Le quartier

kart.yeh   neighborhood

La rue

rü   street

Le bâtiment
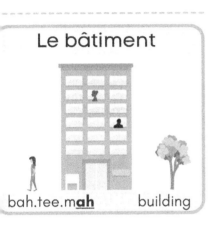
bah.tee.m**ah**   building

L'hôtel (m.)

oh.tel   hotel

L'hôpital (m.)
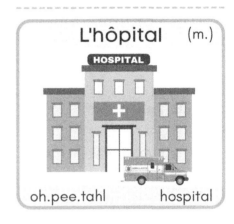
oh.pee.tahl   hospital

La pharmacie
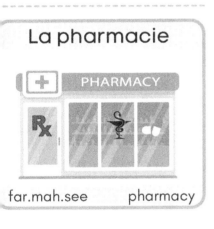
far.mah.see   pharmacy

La banque

b**ah**k   bank

Le parc

park   park

La station de police

stah.sy**oh** duh poh.lees   police station

La mairie

l**ah**g   city hall

L'ambassade (f.)

ah.bah.sad   embassy

► **Connect each English word to its correct translation:**

The city hall	•	L'hôpital
The city	•	La banque
The street	•	L'ambassade
The police station	•	L'hôtel
The bank	•	La pharmacie
The hotel	•	Le bâtiment
The park	•	La mairie
The neighborhood	•	La rue
The hospital	•	La station de police
The embassy	•	Le quartier
The pharmacy	•	Le parc
The building	•	La ville

Translate: By memory only first, then fill in any missing words with help from the previous page.

The bank	The pharmacy	The building
The street	The embassy	The city
The police station	The neighborhood	The city hall
The hotel	The hospital	The park

Les magasins - The shops

Le magasin

mah.gah.z**uh**   store

Le centre commercial

sahtr koh.mair.syahl   mall

Le supermarché

sü.pair mahr.sheh   super-market

Le marché

mahr.sheh   farmer's market

La boulangerie

boo.l**ah**j.ree   bakery

La pâtisserie

pah.tees.ree   pastry shop

La boucherie

boosh.ree   butcher shop

Le restaurant

ress.toh.**rah**   restaurant

Le café

kah.feh   coffee shop

Le salon de coiffure

sah.loh duh kwah.für   hair salon

Le bureau de poste

bü.roh duh post   post office

Le bar

bar   bar

► Connect each English word to its correct translation:

The bakery	•	La boulangerie
The mall	•	Le magasin
The butcher shop	•	Le restaurant
The supermarket	•	Le centre commercial
The store	•	Le bar
The post office	•	La boucherie
The pastry shop	•	Le marché
The hair salon	•	Le salon de coiffure
The restaurant	•	Le café
The bar	•	La pâtisserie
The farmer's market	•	Le bureau de poste
The coffee shop	•	Le supermarché

→ Translate: By memory only first, then fill in any missing words with help from the previous page.

The store	The butcher shop	The pastry shop
_____	_____	_____
The bakery	The mall	The post office
_____	_____	_____
The restaurant	The hair salon	The farmer's market
_____	_____	_____
The supermarket	The coffee shop	The bar
_____	_____	_____

ranslate all the words your remember, check your answers with the word list in p.

New Year's day •

Father's Day •

Happy Father's Day •

Christmas Eve •

New Year's Eve •

Merry Christmas •

Public holiday •

Happy Mother's Day •

Christmas •

Mother's Day •

Easter •

Happy New Year •

The ball •

The gift card •

The video game •

The instrument •

The board game •

The robot •

The stuffed animal •

The bicycle •

The doll •

The gaming console •

The toy •

The jewelry •

The high school •

The middle school •

The student (child) •

The preschool •

1. The lesson •

2. The university •

3. The homework •

4. The older student •
   (teen & up)

5. The exam •

6. The elemetary •
   school •

7. The nursery •

8. The grades •

9. The blackboard/ •
   whiteboard

10. The glue •

11. The pencil •

12. The classroom •

13. The calculator •

14. The eraser •

15. The notebook •

16. The teacher •

17. The sheet of paper •

18. The pen •

19. The scissors •

20. The book •

21. Algebra •

22. Science •

23. Geography •

24. The foreign •
    language

Vords to review:

Translate all the words your remember, check your answers with the word list in p.

1. Biology •	1. The secretary •
2. Art •	2. The unemployement •
3. Math •	3. To be fired •
4. Physics •	4. The printer •
5. Geometry •	5. The police station •
6. Chemistry •	6. The embassy •
7. Literature •	7. The pharmacy •
8. History •	8. The bank •
9. The lawyer (f.) •	9. The park •
10. The employee •	10. The neighborhood •
11. The accountant •	11. The hotel •
12. The manager •	12. The hospital •
13. The policeman •	13. The building •
14. The doctor •	14. The street •
15. The engineer •	15. The city •
16. The dentist •	16. The city hall •
17. The artist •	17. The supermarket •
18. The firefighter •	18. The store •
19. The nurse (f.) •	19. The pastry shop •
20. The businessman •	20. The hair salon •
21. The director/CEO •	21. The post office •
22. The interview •	22. The restaurant •
23. To be hired •	23. The butcher shop •
24. The computer •	24. The mall •
25. To be retired •	25. The bakery •
26. The colleague •	26. The bar •
27. The meeting •	27. The farmer's market •
28. The salary •	28. The coffee shop •

<u>Words to review</u>:

Les sorties - Outings

Le cinéma

see.neh.mah movie theater

Le musée

mü.zeh   museum

La bibliothèque

bee.blee.oh.tek   library

Le zoo

zoh   zoo

Le cirque

seerk   circus

Le théatre

teh.ahtr   theater

La piscine

pee.seen   swimming pool

La boîte de nuit

bwat duh nüee   nightclub

L'église (f.)
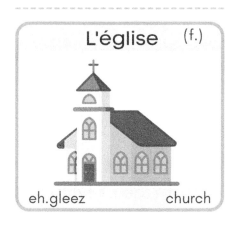
eh.gleez   church

La mosquée

moh.skeh   mosque

La synagogue

see.nah.gog   synagogue

Le temple

t**ah**pl   temple

► **Connect each English word to its correct translation:**

The swimming pool •	Le cinéma
The museum •	Le cirque
The nightclub •	La piscine
The zoo •	L'église
The church •	Le zoo
The circus •	La mosquée
The temple •	La bibliothèque
The movie theater •	La synagogue
The theater •	Le théatre
The synagogue •	La boîte de nuit
The mosque •	Le temple
The library •	Le musée

Translate: By memory only first, then fill in any missing words with help from the previous page.

The mosque	The swimming pool	The church
_____	_____	_____
The library	The temple	The circus
_____	_____	_____
The zoo	The movie theater	The museum
_____	_____	_____
The theater	The synagogue	The nightclub
_____	_____	_____

Les transports - Transportation

La voiture

vwah.tür   car

Le camion

kah.my**oh**   truck

La moto

moh.toh   motorcycle

L'avion (m.)
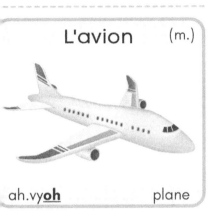
ah.vy**oh**   plane

Le train
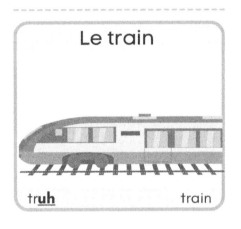
tr**uh**   train

Le vélo

veh.loh   bicycle

Le métro

meh.troh   subway

Le tramway

trahm.way   tramway

Le bus

büs   bus

Le taxi

tak.see   taxi

La station

stah.sy**oh**   station

Le ticket

tee.kay   ticket

➤ **Connect each English word to its correct translation:**

The car	•		La moto
The train	•		L'avion
The motorcycle	•		Le métro
The station	•		Le bus
The tramway	•		La voiture
The ticket	•		Le train
The truck	•		Le taxi
The bus	•		Le tramway
The bicycle	•		Le camion
The taxi	•		Le ticket
The subway	•		Le vélo
The plane	•		Le station

Translate: By memory only first, then fill in any missing words with help from the previous page.

The train	The bicycle	The taxi
The subway	The tramway	The ticket
The plane	The car	The station
The truck	The bus	The motorcycle

La direction - Directions

Les feux de circulation

fuh duh seer.kü.lah.sy**oh**   traffic lights

tourner à droite

toor.neh ah drwat   turn right

tourner à gauche

toor.neh ah goh.sh   turn left

Aller tout droit

ah.leh too drwah   go straight

C'est loin

say lw**uh**   It's far

C'est proche

say prosh   It's close

Le passage piéton

pah.sahj pyeh.t**oh**   pedestrian crossing

Le nord

nor   north

Le sud

süd   south

L'ouest

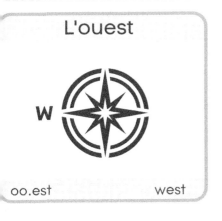

oo.est   west

L'est

est   east

Le demi-tour

duh.mee toor   U-turn

▶ Connect each English word to its correct translation:

Turn right	•	Aller tout droit
South	•	C'est proche
The traffic lights	•	Le passage piéton
Go straight	•	Tourner à droite
The pedestrian crossing	•	L'ouest
Turn left	•	C'est loin
U-turn	•	Le demi-tour
North	•	Tourner à gauche
It's close	•	Le sud
East	•	L'est
West	•	Les feux de circulation
It's far	•	Le nord

Translate: By memory only first, then fill in any missing words with help from the previous page.

Go straight	The traffic lights	South
_____	_____	_____
Turn right	North	Turn left
_____	_____	_____
The pedestrian crossing	It's far	East
_____	_____	_____
U-turn	West	It's close
_____	_____	_____

La banque - The bank

Le compte bancaire

koht bah.kair   bank account

Le chéquier

sheh.kyeh   checkbook

Le chèque

shayk   check

La carte bancaire

kart bah.kair   debit card

Le code PIN

kod peen   pin number/code

Le numéro de carte

nü.meh.roh
duh kart   card number

Le virement bancaire
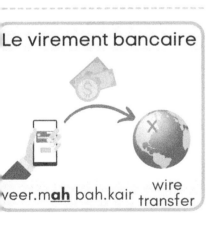
veer.mah bah.kair   wire transfer

Le guichet automatique

ghee.shay
oh.toh.mah.teek   ATM

Le banquier

bahk.yeh   banker

Le client

klee.yah   client

La signature

see.nyah.tür   signature

Le prêt

pray   loan

► Connect each English word to its correct translation:

The bank account •	Le chèque
The card number •	Le virement bancaire
The debit card •	Le banquier
The wire transfer •	Le compte bancaire
The pin number /code •	Le prêt
The checkbook •	Le code (pin)
The banker •	Le guichet automatique
The client •	La carte bancaire
The ATM •	Le client
The signature •	Le numéro de carte
The loan •	Le chéquier
The check •	La signature

● **Translate:** By memory only first, then fill in any missing words with help from the previous page.

The signature	The pin number/code	The check
The loan	The wire transfer	The client
The checkbook	The bank account	The debit card
The card number	The ATM	The banker

Le courrier - The mail

Le courrier

koo.ryeh   mail

La lettre

letr   letter

L'enveloppe (f.)

ah.vuh.lop   envelope

Le timbre

t**uh**br   stamp

Le colis

koh.lee   package

Le postier

poh.styeh   mailman

La boîte aux lettres

bwat oh letr   mailbox

La carte postale

kart post.tahl   postcard

La facture

fahk.tür   bill

L'adresse

ah.dress   address

La livraison

lee.vreh.z**oh**   delivery

La publicité

püb.lee.see.teh   ads

➤ Connect each English word to its correct translation:

The stamp	Le postier
The mailman	Le timbre
The mail	La facture
The postcard	La lettre
The package	La livraison
The ads	Le colis
The envelope	La boîte aux lettres
The mailbox	Le courrier
The letter	La publicité
The delivery	L'enveloppe
The address	La carte postale
The bill	L'adresse

➔ Translate: By memory only first, then fill in any missing words with help from the previous page.

The letter	The postcard	The ads
_____	_____	_____
The package	The stamp	The envelope
_____	_____	_____
The mailbox	The mail	The delivery
_____	_____	_____
The bill	The address	The mailman
_____	_____	_____

Au parc - At the park

L'herbe (f.)
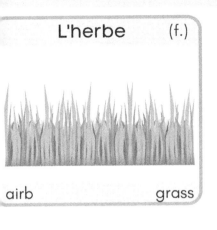
airb   grass

L'arbre (m.)

ahr.br   tree

Les fleurs (f.)
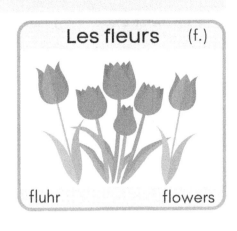
fluhr   flowers

Les insectes (m.)
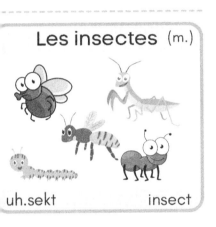
uh.sekt   insect

L'aire de jeu (f.)

air duh juh   playground

La fontaine

f**oh**.ten   fountain

Les enfants (m.)

ah.f**ah**   children

Le banc

b**ah**   bench

Le pigeon

pee.j**oh**   pigeon

Le bac à sable

bahk ah sahbl   sandbox

La balançoire

bah.**lah**.swahr   swing

Le toboggan

toh.boh.g**ah**   slide

Connect each English word to its correct translation:

The fountain	•	L'arbre
The pigeon	•	Le pigeon
The insect	•	La fontaine
The bench	•	Les fleurs
The flowers	•	Le banc
The playground	•	Les enfants
The swing	•	Le toboggan
The grass	•	L'herbe
The children	•	L'aire de jeu
The tree	•	La balançoire
The slide	•	Le bac à sable
The sandbox	•	Les insectes

Translate: By memory only first, then fill in any missing words with help from the previous page.

The tree	The slide	The swing
The playground	The flowers	The insect
The grass	The pigeon	The sandbox
The children	The bench	The fountain

Les activités au parc - Park activities

Jouer

joo.eh — To play

Faire du vélo

fair dü veh.loh — Ride a bike

Faire du roller

fair dü roh.luhr — Roller blading

Se promener

suh pro.muh.neh — To go for a walk

Promener le chien

pro.muh.neh luh shy**uh** — walk the dog

Courir

koo.reer — Run

Faire un pique-nique

fair **uh** peek.neek — have a picnic

Discuter

dees.kü.teh — Talk/chitchat

Se relaxer

suh ruh.lak.seh — relax

Lire un livre

leer **uh** leevr — read a book

Faire du sport

fair dü spor — To exercise

Pêcher

peh.sheh — To fish

Ride a bike	•	Pêcher
Have a picnic	•	Se promener
To fish	•	Faire du sport
To go for a walk	•	Jouer
Walk the dog	•	Faire un pique-nique
Read a book	•	Se relaxer
To play	•	Faire du vélo
To exercise	•	Promener le chien
Roller blading	•	Lire un livre
To run	•	Faire du roller
Talk/chitchat	•	Courir
Relax	•	Discuter

⟳ **Translate:** By memory only first, then fill in any missing words with help from the previous page.

Walk the dog	To play	To fish
Have a picnic	Relax	Run
To go for a walk	Read a book	Roller blading
To exercise	Talk/chitchat	Ride a bike

Le parc d'attraction - The amusement park

Le parc d'attraction

park
dah.trahk.sy**oh**

amusement park

Le guichet

ghee.shay   ticket booth

Les montagne russes
(f.)
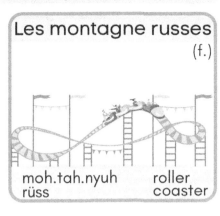
moh.tah.nyuh rüss

roller coaster

La grande roue
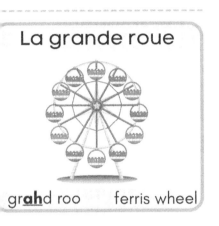
gr**ah**d roo   ferris wheel

Les autos-tamponneuses (f.)

oh.toh t**ah**.poh.nuhz

bumper cars

Les jeux d'arcade
(m.)

juh dahr.kahd   arcade games

Le manège

mah.nehj   carousel

Le beignet

beh.nyeh   donut

La limonade

lee.moh.nad   lemonade

La barbe à papa

barb ah pa.pa cotton candy

La glaçe

glass   ice cream

La pomme d'amour

pom dah.moor candy apple

▶ <u>**Connect each English word to its correct translation:**</u>

The amusement park •	La grande roue
The carousel •	Le beignet
The roller coaster •	Les autos-tamponneuses
The cotton candy •	Le manège
The ice cream •	Le guichet
The bumper cars •	La barbe à papa
The lemonade •	La glaçe
The donut •	Les montagnes russes
The ferris wheel •	La pomme d'amour
The candy apple •	Les jeux d'arcade
The arcade games •	Le parc d'attraction
The ticket booth •	La limonade

Translate: By memory only first, then fill in any missing words with help from the previous page.

The ticket booth	The carousel	The cotton candy
The arcade games	The roller coaster	The ice cream
The candy apple	The lemonade	The donut
The ferris wheel	The bumper cars	The amusement park

Le paysage - The landscape

La mer
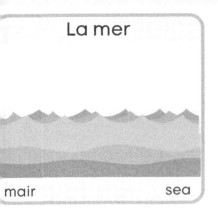
mair   sea

La montagne

m**oh**.tah.nyuh   mountain

La forêt

for.ray   forest

Le bois
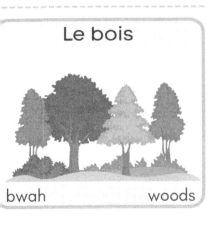
bwah   woods

La rivière

reev.yair   river

Le lac

lahk   lake

Le désert

deh.zair   desert

Le volcan

vohl.k**ah**   volcano

La chute d'eau

shüt doh   waterfall

La falaise

fah.layz   cliff

L'île (f.)

eel   island

Les pierres (f.)

pyair   rocks

► **Connect each English word to its correct translation:**

The lake	L'île
The woods	La mer
The volcano	Le lac
The sea	La chute d'eau
The island	La rivière
The desert	La forêt
The forest	Le volcan
The rocks	La falaise
The waterfall	La montagne
The mountain	Les pierres
The cliff	Le bois
The river	Le désert

→ **Translate:** By memory only first, then fill in any missing words with help from the previous page.

The sea	The volcano	The mountain
___	___	___
The woods	The river	The waterfall
___	___	___
The cliff	The island	The lake
___	___	___
The desert	The forest	The rocks
___	___	___

Translate all the words your remember, check your answers with the word list in p.

A		B	
1. The zoo	•	1. Go straight	•
2. The synagogue	•	2. East	•
3. The mosque	•	3. West	•
4. The church	•	4. The pedestrian crossing	•
5. The temple	•	5. U-turn	•
6. The movie theater	•	6. North	•
7. The circus	•	7. Turn left	•
8. The theater	•	8. It's close	•
9. The library	•	9. It's far	•
10. The nightclub	•	10. The wire transfer	•
11. The museum	•	11. The signature	•
12. The swimming pool		12. The loan	•
13. The station		13. The pin number /code	•
14. The taxi	•	14. The banker	•
15. The subway	•	15. The client	•
16. The tramway	•	16. The checkbook	•
17. The truck	•	17. The ATM	•
18. The bus	•	18. The check	•
19. The ticket	•	19. The debit card	•
20. The bicycle	•	20. The card number	•
21. The plane	•	21. The bank account	•
22. The motorcycle	•	22. The postcard	•
23. The train	•	23. The package	•
24. The car	•	24. The mail	•
25. The traffic lights	•	25. The mailman	•
26. South	•	26. The stamp	•
27. Turn right	•		
	•		

Words to review:

Translate all the words your remember, check your answers with the word list in p.

A	B
1. The delivery •	1. Talk/chitchat •
2. The address •	2. Roller blading •
3. The envelope •	3. Relax •
4. The mailbox •	4. The cotton candy •
5. The ads •	5. The candy apple •
6. The letter •	6. The arcade games •
7. The bill •	7. The ice cream •
8. The bench •	8. The lemonade •
9. The tree •	9. The donut •
10. The slide •	10. The bumper cars •
11. The flowers •	11. The ferris wheel •
12. The swing •	12. The ticket booth •
13. The grass •	13. The roller coaster •
14. The playground •	14. The carousel •
15. The children •	15. The amusement •
16. The sandbox •	park
17. The insect •	16. The sea •
18. The pigeon •	17. The mountain •
19. The fountain •	18. The cliff •
20. To go for a walk •	19. The island •
21. Walk the dog •	20. The forest •
22. To play •	21. The rocks •
23. To exercise •	22. The desert •
24. Read a book •	23. The waterfall •
25. To fish •	24. The river •
26. Have a picnic •	25. The volcano •
27. Ride a bike •	26. The woods •
28. To run •	27. The lake •

Words to review:

Les vacances - The vacation

L'aéroport (m.)

ah.eh.roh.por airport

Le vol
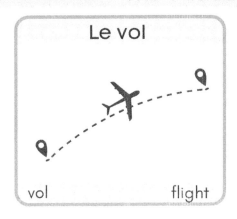
vol flight

Le billet d'avion

bee.yeh dah.vy**oh** plane ticket

Le départ

deh.pahr departure

L'arrivée (f.)

ah.ree.veh arrival

La valise

vah.leez luggage/suitcase

Le bagage à main

bah.gahj ah m**uh** carry-on

Le / la touriste

too.reest tourist

La voiture de location

vwah.tür duh loh.kah.sy**oh** rental car

La chambre d'hôtel

sh**ah**br doh.tel hotel room

La carte

kart map

Le passeport

pass.por passport

▶ **Connect each English word to its correct translation:**

The tourist •	L'arrivée
The departure •	La valise
The airport •	Le billet d'avion
The arrival •	Le bagage à main
The map •	L'aéroport
The flight •	Le passeport
The passport •	Le vol
The suitcase •	La chambre d'hôtel
The hotel room •	Le départ
The car rental •	La carte
The plane ticket •	La voiture de location
The carry-on •	Le touriste

⊙ Baggages/luggages also: Les bagages (bah.gahj)

⇒ **Translate:** By memory only first, then fill in any missing words with help from the previous page.

The car rental	The tourist	The arrival
_____	_____	_____
The plane ticket	The carry-on	The hotel room
_____	_____	_____
The suitcase	The flight	The passport
_____	_____	_____
The airport	The departure	The map
_____	_____	_____

La plage - The beach

La plage

plahj   beach

Le parasol

pah.rah.sol   beach umbrella

La serviette de plage

sair.vyet duh plahj   beach towel

La chaise de plage

shayz duh plahj   beach chair

Le maillot de bain

mah.yoh duh b**uh**   swimsuit

Les lunettes de soleil (f.)

lü.net duh soh.ley   sunglasses

La crème solaire

krem soh.lair   sunscreen

L'appareil photo (m.)

ah.pah.rey foh.toh   camera

Le goûter (snack)

goo.teh   snack

La vague

vahg   wave

La bouée

boo.eh   buoy/floaty

Le sable

sahbl   sand

► Connect each English word to its correct translation:

The sunglasses •	La chaise de plage
The beach chair •	La vague
The snack •	La serviette de plage
The beach umbrella •	L'appareil photo
The sunscreen •	Le maillot de bain
The beach towel •	Le goûter (snack)
The camera •	Le parasol
The swimsuit •	Les lunettes de soleil
The wave •	La bouée
The beach •	Le sable
The buoy / floaty •	La plage
The sand •	La crème solaire

⊙ **Translate:** By memory only first, then fill in any missing words with help from the previous page.

The snack	The wave	The beach chair
___	___	___
The beach umbrella	The swimsuit	The sand
___	___	___
The sunglasses	The buoy / floaty	The beach
___	___	___
The beach towel	The sunscreen	The camera
___	___	___

La nourriture (1) - The food (1)

Le poisson
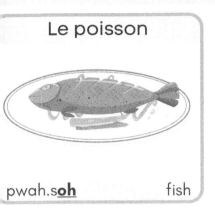
pwah.s**oh**   fish

La viande

vy**ah**d   meat

Le boeuf

buhf   beef

Le poulet

poo.leh   chicken

La dinde

d**uh**nd   turkey

Le porc

por   pork

L'agneau

ah.nyoh   lamb

Les fruits de mer (m.)

früee duh mair   seafood

Le champignon

sh**ah**.pee.ny**oh**   mushroom

Le crabe

krab   crab

La crevette

kruh.vet   shrimp

L'oeuf

uhf   egg

The lamb •	Le porc
The egg •	La viande
The chicken •	L'oeuf
The fish •	Les fruits de mer
The pork •	Le poisson
The seafood •	Le crabe
The shrimp •	La dinde
The turkey •	Le poulet
The mushroom •	La crevette
The meat •	Le champignon
The crab •	Le boeuf
The beef •	L'agneau

(!) The egg: L'oeuf (luhf) / The eggs: Les oeufs (leh zuh) (**F** unpronounced)

Translate: By memory only first, then fill in any missing words with help from the previous page.

The crab	The turkey	The chicken
The fish	The pork	The lamb
The egg	The meat	The beef
The seafood	The salmon	The shrimp

Le riz

ree   rice

Les pâtes

paht   pasta

Les nouilles (f.)

noo.yuh   noodles

Le pain

p**uh**   bread

Les frites (f.)

freet   fries

Les légumes (m.)

leh.güm   vegetables

Les fruits (m.)

früee   fruits

La salade

sah.lahd   salad

La soupe

soop   soup

Les haricots (m.)

ah.ree.koh   beans

Le fromage

froh.mahj   cheese

Le yaourt

yah.oort   yogurt

The beans •	Les haricots
The noodles •	Les nouilles
The cheese •	La soupe
The vegetables •	Le riz
The soup •	La salade
The rice •	Les frites
The fruits •	Les fruits
The pasta •	Le pain
The salad •	Le fromage
The yogurt •	Les pâtes
The bread •	Le yaourt
The fries •	Les légumes

Translate: By memory only first, then fill in any missing words with help from the previous page.

The rice	The bread	The fries
The soup	The noodles	The fruits
The pasta	The vegetables	The beans
The salad	The cheese	The yogurt

Les légumes - The vegetables

La carotte

kah.rot   carrot

La pomme de terre

pom duh tair   potato

La tomate

toh.maht   tomato

Les petits pois (m.)
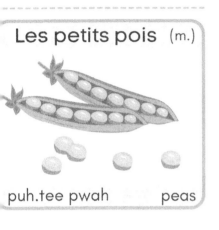
puh.tee pwah   peas

Les haricots verts (m.)

ah.ree.koh vair   green beans

Le concombre

k**oh**.k**oh**br   cucumber

La courgette

koor.jet   zucchini

L'oignon (m.)

oh.ny**oh**   onion

Le maïs

mah.ees   corn

La laitue

lay.tü   lettuce

Le chou-fleur

shoo fluhr   cauliflower

Le poivron

pwah.vr**oh**   bell pepper

The peas •	Le poivron
The cucumber •	La carotte
The corn •	Les petits pois
The carrot •	Le concombre
The cauliflower •	Le maïs
The zucchini •	Le chou-fleur
The tomato •	La pomme de terre
The bell pepper •	La courgette
The lettuce •	La tomate
The potato •	L'oignon
The onion •	Les haricots verts
The green beans •	La laitue

→ **Translate:** By memory only first, then fill in any missing words with help from the previous page.

The green beans	The cauliflower	The potato
The peas	The tomato	The corn
The carrot	The cucumber	The lettuce
The onion	The zucchini	The bell pepper

Les fruits - The fruits

La pomme

pom   apple

L'orange

oh.**rah**j   orange

La banane

bah.nahn   banana

La poire

pwahr   pear

Les raisins (m.)

reh.z**uh**   grapes

L'ananas (m.)

ah.nah.nahs   pineapple

La pêche

pesh   peach

La fraise

frayz   strawberry

La pastèque

pass.tek   watermelon

Les cerises (f.)
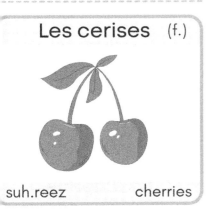
suh.reez   cherries

Le citron

see.tr**oh**   lemon

L'abricot (m.)

ah.bree.koh   apricot

The pineapple •	Les raisins
The strawberry •	L'ananas
The cherries •	L'orange
The banana •	Le citron
The lemon •	Les cerises
The grapes •	La pêche
The apricot •	La fraise
The peach •	La pomme
The watermelon •	La poire
The pear •	L'abricot
The apple •	La pastèque
The orange •	La banane

Translate: By memory only first, then fill in any missing words with help from the previous page.

The strawberry	The pineapple	The apricot
The apple	The peach	The grapes
The cherries	The orange	The lemon
The pear	The banana	The watermelon

Les boissons - The drinks

L'eau (f.)

oh   water

Le lait

lay   milk

Le thé

teh   tea

Le café

kah.feh   coffee

Le café au lait

kah.feh oh lay   latte/coffee with milk

Le chocolat chaud

shoh.koh.lah shoh   hot chocolate

Le smoothie

smoo.tee   smoothie

Le jus

jü   juice

Le soda

soh.dah   soda

L'eau gazeuse (f.)

oh gah.zuhz   sparkly water

L'eau minérale (f.)

oh mee.neh.rahl   mineral water

Les glaçons (m.)

glah.s**oh**   ice cubes

> **Connect each English word to its correct translation:**

The hot chocolate •	Le jus
The coffee •	Les glaçons
The sparkly water •	Le thé
The juice •	Le chocolat chaud
The smoothie •	L'eau gazeuse
The mineral water •	Le lait
The tea •	L'eau
The latte/ coffee with milk •	Le café au lait
The milk •	L'eau minérale
The soda •	Le café
The ice cubes •	Le smoothie
The water •	Le soda

Translate: By memory only first, then fill in any missing words with help from the previous page.

The tea	The hot chocolate	The ice cubes
The sparkly water	The coffee	The water
Latte/coffee with milk	The mineral water	The milk
The juice	The smoothie	The soda

Les repas/ Le petit déjeuner - The meals/ Breakfast

Le petit-déjeuner

puh.tee
deh.juh.neh   breakfast

Le déjeuner

deh.juh.neh   lunch

Le dîner

dee.neh   dinner

La brioche

bree.osh   brioche bread

Le croissant

krwah.s**ah**   croissant

Le pain au chocolat

p**uh** oh   chocolate
shoh.koh.lah   croissant

La tartine

tahr.teen   toast

Les oeufs brouillés (m.)

uh broo.yeh   scrambled eggs

L'omelette (f.)

ohm.let   omelet

Les oeufs aux plats

uh oh plah   sunny side up

Le beurre

buhr   butter

La confiture

k**oh**.fee.tür   jam

➤ Connect each English word to its correct translation:

The croissant •	Le dîner
The breakfast •	L'omelette
The omelet •	La brioche
The toast •	Le pain au chocolat
The butter •	Le beurre
The lunch •	Le petit-déjeuner
Sunny side up eggs •	La confiture
The brioche bread •	Le croissant
The scrambled eggs •	Les oeufs brouillés
The chocolate croissant •	Les oeufs aux plats
The dinner •	La tartine
The jam •	Le déjeuner

⟳ Translate: By memory only first, then fill in any missing words with help from the previous page.

The croissant	The butter	The jam
The omelet	The breakfast	The scrambled eggs
The lunch	The brioche bread	Sunny side up eggs
The dinner	The chocolate croissant	The toast

Les épices et condiments - The spices and condiments

Le sel
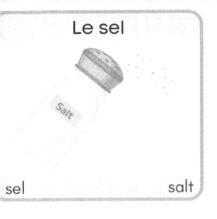
sel   salt

Le poivre

pwahvr   black pepper

Le ketchup

ket.shup   ketchup

La moutarde

moo.tahrd   mustard

La mayonnaise

mah.yoh.naiz   mayonnaise

La sauce (piquante)

sohs (pee.**kah**t)   (hot) sauce

L'huile (f.)
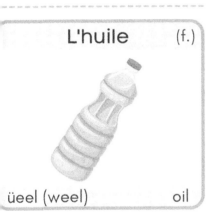
üeel (weel)   oil

L'huile d'olive (f.)

üeel doh.leev   olive oil

La vinaigrette

vee.neh.gret   salad dressing

Le miel

myehl   honey

Les cacahuètes (f.)

kah.kah.wet   peanuts

Les amandes (f.)

ah.m**ah**d   almonds

► **Connect each English word to its correct translation:**

The mustard	•	Le ketchup
The oil	•	L'huile
The peanuts	•	Le sel
The olive oil	•	La sauce (piquante)
The salt	•	Le miel
The (hot) sauce	•	La moutarde
The almonds	•	La vinaigrette
The black pepper	•	Les cacahuètes
The honey	•	Le poivre
The mayonnaise	•	L'huile d'olive
The ketchup	•	Les amandes
The salad dressing	•	La mayonnaise

◐ **Translate:** By memory only first, then fill in any missing words with help from the previous page.

The (hot) sauce	The mayonnaise	The mustard
The salt	The oil	The honey
The salad dressing	The black pepper	The ketchup
The almonds	The olive oil	The peanuts

Translate all the words your remember, check your answers with the word list in p.

.The arrival	•		1. The fish	•	
.The car rental	•		2. The meat	•	
.The plane ticket	•		3. The crab	•	
.The map	•		4. The pork	•	
.The passport	•		5. The shrimp	•	
.The suitcase	•		6. The turkey	•	
.The flight	•		7. The seafood	•	
.The hotel room	•		8. The mushroom	•	
.The carry-on	•		9. The beef	•	
.The airport	•		10. The vegetables	•	
.The departure	•		11. The yogurt	•	
.The tourist	•		12. The bread	•	
.The beach	•		13. The soup	•	
umbrella	•		14. The fruits	•	
.The beach	•		15. The pasta	•	
.The buoy / floaty	•		16. The rice	•	
.The sunscreen	•		17. The salad	•	
.The camera	•		18. The fries	•	
.The swimsuit	•		19. The cheese	•	
.The beach towel	•		20. The noodles	•	
.The wave	•		21. The beans	•	
.The sand	•		22. The carrot	•	
.The snack	•		23. The cauliflower	•	
.The beach chair	•		24. The zucchini	•	
.The sunglasses	•		25. The corn	•	
.The chicken	•		26. The cucumber	•	
.The egg	•		27. The peas	•	
.The lamb	•				

Words to review:

Translate all the words your remember, check your answers with the word list in p.

1. The potato •
2. The onion •
3. The tomato •
4. The bell pepper •
5. The lettuce •
6. The green beans •
7. The banana •
8. The pear •
9. The apple •
10. The lemon •
11. The apricot •
12. The peach •
13. The grapes •
14. The watermelon •
15. The orange •
16. The cherries •
17. The strawberry •
18. The pineapple •
19. The juice •
20. The smoothie •
21. The tea •
22. The latte/coffee •
    with milk •
23. The mineral water •
24. The milk •
25. The sparkly water •
26. The coffee •
27. The hot chocolate •

1. The soda •
2. The ice cubes •
3. The water •
4. The toast •
5. The chocolate
   croissant •
6. The dinner •
7. The butter •
8. Sunny side up eggs •
9. The brioche bread •
10. The lunch •
11. The scrambled eggs •
12. The jam •
13. The omelet •
14. The breakfast •
15. The croissant •
16. The olive oil •
17. The mayonnaise •
18. The ketchup •
19. The salt •
20. The almonds •
21. The black pepper •
22. The (hot) sauce •
23. The honey •
24. The salad dressing •
25. The peanuts •
26. The oil •
27. The mustard •

Words to review:

Les snacks et sucreries - Snacks and sweets

Le gâteau

gah.toh   cake

La tarte

tart   pie

Les bonbons (m.)

b**oh**.b**oh**   candies

Le chocolat

shoh.koh.lah   chocolate

Le biscuit

bees.kwee   cookie

La glace

glass   ice cream

Les chips

sheeps   chips

Les noix

nwah   nuts/walnuts

La barre de céréales

bahr duh seh.reh.ahl   cereal bar

La gaufre

gohfr   waffle

La pâtisserie

pah.tee.suh.ree   pastry

Le pudding/flan

poo.ding / fla**h**   pudding

Connect each English word to its correct translation:

The pie •	La tarte
The candies •	La pâtisserie
The cookie •	Le gâteau
The cake •	La barre de céréales
The pastry •	Le chocolat
The chips •	Le pudding/flan
The nuts/walnuts •	Les bonbons
The ice cream •	Les noix
The pudding •	La gaufre
The cereal bar •	Les chips
The chocolate •	La glace
The waffle •	Le biscuit

Translate: By memory only first, then fill in any missing words with help from the previous page.

The cereal bar	The chocolate	The pastry
The pudding	The candies	The pie
The chips	The nuts/walnuts	The waffle
The cake	The ice cream	The cookie

Au restaurant - At the restaurant

Le serveur

sair.vuhr — waiter

La nourriture

noo.ree.tür — food

Le menu

muh.nü — menu

La paille

pah.yuh — straw

L'entrée (f.)

ah.treh — appetizer

Le plat principal

plah pr**uh**.see.pahl — main course

Le dessert

deh.sair — dessert

Le cuisinier/chef

küee.zee.nyeh — cook/chef

Le pourboire

poor.bwahr — tip

L'addition (f.)
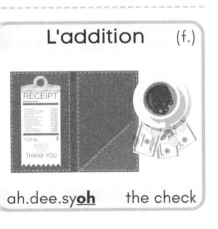
ah.dee.sy**oh** — the check

Avoir faim

ah.vwahr f**uh** — To be hungry

Commander

koh.m**ah**·deh — To order

➤ **Connect each English word to its correct translation:**

The menu	•	L'addition
The food	•	Commander
The cook/chef	•	La paille
The main course	•	Le serveur
The check	•	Avoir faim
The straw	•	L'entrée
To order	•	Le dessert
The appetizer	•	La nourriture
To be hungry	•	Le cuisinier/chef
The tip	•	Le pourboire
The waiter	•	Le menu
The dessert	•	Le plat principal

(!) The wait**ress** : la serv**euse** (sair.vuhz)

◯ **Translate:** By memory only first, then fill in any missing words with help from the previous page.

The dessert	The food	To order
The tip	The main course	The check
The waiter	The menu	The cook/chef
The appetizer	To be hungry	The straw

Au supermarché - At the supermarket

Le caissier

kess.yeh — cashier

La caisse

kess — cash register

Le caddie

kah.dee — shopping cart

Le panier

pah.nyeh — basket

Le reçu

ruh.sü — receipt

Le rayon

reh.**yoh** — (store) aisle

Les surgelés (m.)

sür.juh.leh — frozen foods

Les boissons (f.)

bwah.**soh** — drinks

Les produits (m.)

pro.dwee — products

Les magazines

mah.gah.zeen — magazines

Acheter

ah.shuh.teh — To buy

Payer

peh.yeh — To pay

► **Connect each English word to its correct translation:**

The receipt	Les surgelés
The shopping cart	Le reçu
The (shopping) basket	Les magazines
To pay	Le rayon
The cashier	Le panier
To buy	Acheter
The products	Les boissons
The frozen foods	Payer
The drinks	Le caissier
The cash register	Les produits
The magazines	Le caddie
The (store) aisle	La caisse

(!) The cashier (fem.) : la caissière (kess.yair)

→ **Translate:** By memory only first, then fill in any missing words with help from the previous page.

The products	The receipt	The drinks
The cashier	The (store) aisle	The cash register
The frozen foods	The (shopping) basket	To pay
The shopping cart	The magazines	To buy

Au centre commercial - At the mall

Les boutiques (f.)

boo.teek   (small) shops

Le parking

pahr.king   parking

L'escalateur (m.)

ehs.kah.lah.tuhr   escalator

Les gens (m.)

j**ah**   people

Les soldes (f.)

sold   Sales

La remise

ruh.meez   discount

Le vendeur

v**ah**.duhr   salesperson (m.)

La foule

fool   crowd

Le bébé

beh.beh   baby

La poucette

poo.set   stroller

Le salon de beauté

sah.l**oh** duh boh.teh   beauty salon

L'agent de sécurité (m.)

ah.j**ah** duh seh.kü.ree.teh   security agent

➤ Connect each English word to its correct translation:

The discount	•	L'escalateur
The escalator	•	Les soldes
The salesperson (m.)	•	Les boutiques
The stroller	•	La foule
The (small) shops	•	Le bébé
The baby	•	La remise
The crowd	•	Le salon de beauté
The parking	•	Le parking
The security agent	•	L'agent de sécurité
The people	•	Le vendeur
Sales	•	La poucette
The beauty salon	•	Les gens

(!) The salesperson (fem.) : la vendeu**se** (v**ah**.duhz)

Translate: By memory only first, then fill in any missing words with help from the previous page.

The security agent	The (small) shops	The stroller
The parking	The discount	Sales
The people	The salesperson (f.)	The crowd
The baby	The escalator	The beauty salon

À l'hôpital - At the hospital

Le patient (m.)

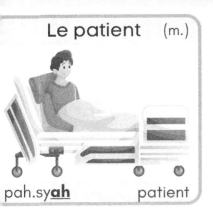

pah.sy**ah**   patient

La santé

s**ah**.teh   health

La maladie

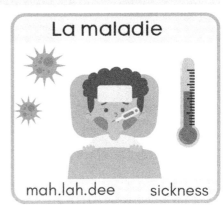

mah.lah.dee   sickness

La blessure

bleh.sür   injury

La brûlure

brü.lür   burn

Le mal de tête

mahl duh tet   headache

Le rhume

rüm   cold (sick)

La fièvre

fyay.vruh   fever

Le mal de gorge

mahl duh gorj   sore throat

La toux

too   cough

La douleur

doo.luhr   pain

Mal au ventre

mahl oh v**ah**tr   stomachache

► <u>Connect each English word to its correct translation:</u>

The injury •	La fièvre
The sickness •	Le patient
The sore throat •	La blessure
The cold (sick) •	Le rhume
The patient (m.) •	La douleur
The pain •	La toux
The health •	La maladie
The cough •	Mal au ventre
The burn •	Le mal de tête
Stomachache •	Le mal de gorge
The fever •	La brûlure
The headache •	La santé

(!) The patient (fem.) : la patiente   (pah.sy<u>ah</u>t)

→ <u>Translate:</u> By memory only first, then fill in any missing words with help from the previous page.

The burn	The pain	The fever
The cough	The injury	The stomachache
The sickness	The cold (sick)	The patient (f.)
The health	The headache	The sore throat

Le traitement (médical) - The (medical) treatment

Le rendez-vous

ah.deh.voo   appointment

La radiographie (radio)
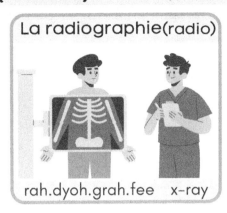
rah.dyoh.grah.fee   x-ray

Le masque

mask   mask

L'ordonnance (f.)
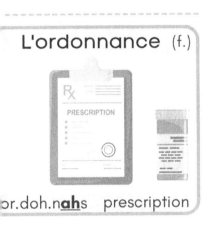
or.doh.n**ah**s   prescription

La piqûre
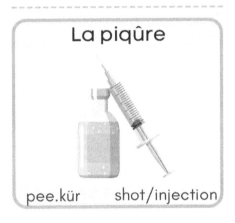
pee.kür   shot/injection

Le pansement

p**ah**s.m**ah**   bandage

Le médicament

neh.dee.kah.m**ah**   medication

La chirurgie

shee.rür.jee   surgery

La pillule
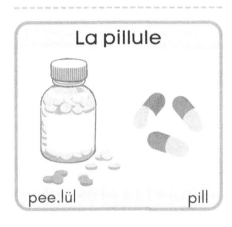
pee.lül   pill

Le syrop

see.roh   syrup

Les gouttes

goot   drops

L'ambulance

ah.bü.**lah**s   ambulance

► **Connect each English word to its correct translation:**

The x-ray	•	La pillule
The syrup	•	La radiographie
The mask	•	Le pansement
The bandage	•	La chirurgie
The ambulance	•	Le rendez-vous
The surgery	•	Le médicament
The shot/injection	•	Les gouttes
The appointment	•	L'ambulance
The drops	•	Le masque
The prescription	•	Le syrop
The pill	•	L'ordonnance
The medication	•	La piqûre

Translate: By memory only first, then fill in any missing words with help from the previous page.

The syrup	The mask	The ambulance
The pill	The shot/injection	The drops
The appointment	The x-ray	The medication
The bandage	The prescription	The surgery

Les valeurs - Values

La gentillesse

ah.tee.yess   kindness

Le respect

ress.peh   respect

La patience

pah.sy**ah**s   patience

La responsabilité

rehs.p**oh**.sah.bee.lee.teh   responsibility

La tolérance

toh.leh.r**ah**s   tolerance

La gratitude

grah.tee.tüd   gratitude

L'honnêteté (f.)

oh.nayt.teh   honesty

La fidelité

fee.day.lee.teh   loyalty

La confiance

k**oh**f.y**ah**s   trust

Le courage

koo.rahj   courage

La générosité

jeh.neh.roh.zee.teh   generosity

La détermination

deh.tair.mee.nah.sy**oh**   determination

► Connect each English word to its correct translation:

The kindness •	Le respect
Loyalty •	L'honnêteté
Responsibility •	La confiance
Gratitude •	La patience
Tolerance •	La générosité
Courage •	La fidelité
Respect •	La responsabilité
Generosity •	La détermination
Trust •	La gentillesse
Patience •	La gratitude
Honesty •	Le courage
Determination •	La tolérance

Translate: By memory only first, then fill in any missing words with help from the previous page.

Kindness	Courage	Generosity
Determination	Responsibility	Loyalty
Patience	Tolerance	Trust
Honesty	Respect	Gratitude

Les activités quotidiennes - The daily activities (Verbs 1)

Travailler

trah.vah.yeh — To work

Manger

m**ah**.jeh — To eat

Sortir

sor.teer — To go out

Faire du shopping

fair dü shoh.peeng — To shop

Se reposer

ruh.poh.zeh — To rest

Parler au téléphone

pahr.leh oh teh.leh.fon — To talk on the phone

Regarder la télé

ruh.gahr.deh lah teh.leh — To watch TV

Cuisiner

kwee.zee.neh — To cook

Dormir

dor.meer — To sleep

Se réveiller

suh reh.veh.yeh — To wake up

Se doucher

suh doo.sheh — To shower

S'habiller

sah.bee.yeh — To get dressed

► **Connect each English word to its correct translation:**

To sleep	Regarder la télé
To wake up	Cuisiner
To shower	Se doucher
To get dressed	S'habiller
To cook	Sortir
To eat	Parler au téléphone
To go out	Manger
To work	Se réveiller
To shop	Faire du shopping
To talk on the phone	Dormir
To rest	Travailler
To watch TV	Se reposer

→ **Translate:** By memory only first, then fill in any missing words with help from the previous page.

To work	To eat	To shop
To rest	To sleep	To watch TV
To shower	To talk on the phone	To go out
To cook	To get dressed	To wake up

Verbes (2) - Verbs (2)

Parler

pahr.leh — To speak/Talk

Boire

bwahr — To drink

Voir

vwahr — To see

Faire

fair — To do

Donner

doh.neh — To give

Prendre

pr**ah**dr — To take

Marcher

mahr.sheh — To walk

Ouvrir

oov.reer — To open

Fermer

fair.meh — To close

Lire

leer — To read

Écrire

eh.kreer — To write

Penser

p**ah**•seh — To think

► Connect each English word to its correct translation:

To do	•	Voir
To write	•	Prendre
To drink	•	Faire
To open	•	Penser
To see	•	Donner
To think	•	Écrire
To give	•	Parler
To walk	•	Ouvrir
To speak/Talk	•	Lire
To read	•	Boire
To take	•	Fermer
To close	•	Marcher

Translate: By memory only first, then fill in any missing words with help from the previous page.

To open	To write	To close
To speak/Talk	To give	To see
To think	To read	To walk
To take	To do	To drink

Translate all the words your remember, check your answers with the word list in p.

A		B	
.The cake	•	1. To pay	•
.The cereal bar	•	2. The cash register	•
.The chocolate	•	3. The magazines	•
.The pastry	•	4. The cashier (f.)	•
.The nuts/walnuts	•	5. The products	•
.The ice cream	•	6. The frozen foods	•
.The chips	•	7. To buy	•
.The pudding	•	8. The drinks	•
.The waffle	•	9. The (store) aisle	•
.The cookie	•	10. The stroller	•
.The pie	•	11. The people	•
.The candies	•	12. The sales	•
.The main course	•	13. The (small) shops	•
.The tip	•	14. The crowd	•
.The waiter	•	15. The parking	•
.The check	•	16. The baby	•
.To order	•	17. The security agent	•
.The appetizer	•	18. The beauty salon	•
.The straw	•	19. The salesperson (m.)	•
.To be hungry	•	20. The escalator	•
.The dessert	•	21. The discount	•
.The cook/chef	•	22. The cold (sick)	•
.The menu	•	23. The patient (m.)	•
.The food	•	24. The pain	•
.The shopping cart	•	25. The sore throat	•
.The receipt	•	26. The sickness	•
.The (shopping) basket	•	27. The injury	•

Words to review:

Translate all the words your remember, check your answers with the word list in p.

A	B
1. The stomachache •	1. Patience •
2. The fever •	2. Honesty •
3. The health •	3. Determination •
4. The cough •	4. To get dressed •
5. The burn •	5. To talk on the •
6. The headache •	phone
7. The bandage •	6. To rest •
8. The prescription •	7. To cook •
9. The pill •	8. To go out •
10. The ambulance •	9. To work •
11. The shot/injection •	10. To eat •
12. The appointment •	11. To shop •
13. The surgery •	12. To watch TV •
14. The drops •	13. To shower •
15. The medication •	14. To wake up •
16. The mask •	15. To sleep •
17. The syrup •	16. To open •
18. The x-ray •	17. To read •
19. Gratitude •	18. To take •
20. Tolerance •	19. To see •
21. Respect •	20. To give •
22. Generosity •	21. To walk •
23. Courage •	22. To think •
24. Responsibility •	23. To speak/Talk •
25. Loyalty •	24. To close •
26. The kindness •	25. To drink •
27. Trust •	26. To write •
	27. To do •

Words to review:

Verbes (3) - Verbs (3)

Danser

d**ah**.seh   To dance

Chanter

sh**ah**.teh   To sing

Trouver

troo.veh   To find

Entendre
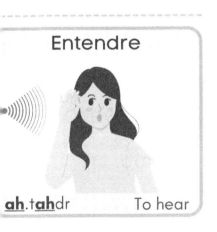
ah.**tah**dr   To hear

Écouter

eh.koo.teh   To listen

Arrêter

ah.reh.teh   To stop

Rire

reer   To laugh

Pleurer

pluh.reh   To cry

Nettoyer

neh.twah.yeh   To clean

Laver

lah.veh   To wash

Charger

shahr.jeh   To charge

Télécharger

teh.leh.shahr.jeh   To download

► Connect each English word to its correct translation:

To sing	•	Entendre
To cry	•	Écouter
To dance	•	Arrêter
To clean	•	Laver
To wash	•	Charger
To hear	•	Télécharger
To listen	•	Nettoyer
To find	•	Pleurer
To charge	•	Rire
To download	•	Trouver
To laugh	•	Chanter
To stop	•	Danser

Translate: By memory only first, then fill in any missing words with help from the previous page.

To cry	To stop	To hear
To listen	To sing	To wash
To download	To charge	To clean
To laugh	To dance	To find

Verbes (4) - Verbs (4)

Réparer

reh.pah.reh — To repair

Casser

kah.seh — To break

Couper

koo.peh — To cut

Préparer

preh.pah.reh — To prepare

Jouer

joo.eh — To play

Demander

duh.m**ah**.deh — To ask

Rêver

reh.veh — To dream

Nager

nah.jeh — To swim

Croire

krwahr — To believe

Choisir

shwah.zeer — To choose

Pouvoir

poo.vwahr — To be able to/Can

Devoir

duh.vwahr — To have to/Must

▶ Connect each English word to its correct translation:

To swim	•	Choisir
To cut	•	Réparer
To have to/Must	•	Pouvoir
To break	•	Préparer
To play	•	Pouvoir
To repair	•	Jouer
To prepare	•	Casser
To be able to/Can	•	Nager
To ask	•	Rêver
To dream	•	Couper
To choose	•	Croire
To believe	•	Demander

Translate: By memory only first, then fill in any missing words with help from the previous page.

To play	To be able to/Can	To dream
To have to/Must	To cut	To repair
To choose	To swim	To break
To play	To prepare	To ask

Verbes (5) - Verbs (5)

Appeler

ah.puh.leh   To call

Répondre

reh.p**oh**dr   To answer

Vendre

v**ah**dr   To sell

Finir

fee.neer   To finish

Tomber

t**oh**.beh   To fall

Crier

kree.yeh   To scream

Vivre
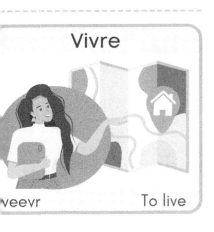
veevr   To live

Monter

m**oh**.teh   To go up

Descendre

deh.s**ah**dr   To go down

Commencer

koh.m**ah**.seh   To start

Attendre

ah.t**ah**dr   To wait

Voyager

vwah.yah.jeh   To travel

> **Connect each English word to its correct translation:**

To go down	Crier
To call	Descendre
To fall	Finir
To wait	Commencer
To sell	Attendre
To finish	Appeler
To go up	Monter
To answer	Vivre
To start	Répondre
To scream	Tomber
To travel	Voyager
To live	Vendre

Translate: By memory only first, then fill in any missing words with help from the previous page.

To call	To finish	To travel
To go down	To start	To fall
To answer	To sell	To wait
To go up	To scream	To live

Les adjectifs (1) - Adjectives (1) (Masc./Fem.)

Gentil/Gentille

j**ah**.tee   Nice/Kind

Méchant / Méchante

meh.sh**ah**/meh.sh**ah**t   Mean

Amusant/Amusante

ah.müs.**ah**/ah.mü.s**ah**t   Fun

Ennuyeux/Ennuyeuse

ah.nwee.yuh
ah.nwee.yuhz   Boring

Grand/Grande

gr**ah**/gr**ah**d   Big/Tall

Petit/Petite
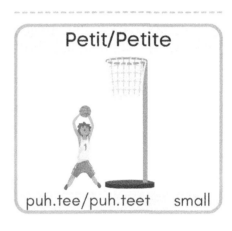
puh.tee/puh.teet   small

Propre

propr   Clean

Sale

sahl   Dirty

Vieux/Vieille

vyuh/vyey   Old

Sympa

s**uh**.pah   Friendly

Gros/Grosse

groh/grohs   Big/Fat

Jeune

juhn   Young

► Connect each English word to its correct translation:

Boring	Gros/Grosse
Mean	Propre
Clean	Méchant/Méchante
Big/Fat	Grand/Grande
Nice/Kind	Gentil/Gentille
Old	Petit/Petite
Young	Vieux/Vieille
Big/Tall	Amusant/Amusante
Fun	Sale
Dirty	Jeune
Friendly	Ennuyeux/Ennuyeuse
Small	Sympa

In French, adjectives agree with the noun (or pronoun) they modify. (Fem./Masc./Sing./Plural)
Some adjectives remain the same in the masculine and feminine form.

Translate: By memory only first, then fill in any missing words with help from the previous page. *(Gender in parenthesis)*

Old (m.)	Nice/Kind (f.)	Small (m.)
Mean (m.)	Clean	Big/Tall (f.)
Dirty	Boring (m.)	Big/Fat (m.)
Fun (m.)	Young	Friendly

Les adjectifs (2) - Adjectives (2) (Masc./Fem.)

Facile

fah.seel — Easy

Difficile

dee.fee.seel — Difficult

Intelligent / Intelligente

uh.teh.lee.**jah**/ja**ht** — Smart

Stupide / bête

stü.peed / bet — Stupid

Fort / Forte

for/fort — Strong

Faible

fay.bl_{uh} — Weak

Rapide
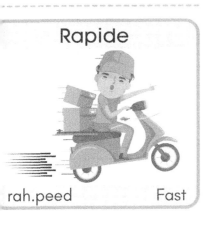
rah.peed — Fast

Lent / Lente

l**ah**/l**ah**t — Slow

Sec / sèche

sayk/saysh — Dry

Mouillé / Mouillée

moo.yeh — Wet

Beau / Belle

boh/bel — Beautiful

Moche

mosh — Ugly

Connect each English word to its correct translation:

Smart	Stupide
Wet	Intelligent/ Intelligente
Easy	Moche
Slow	Rapide
Strong	Beau/Belle
Dry	Facile
Stupid	Faible
Fast	Lent/Lente
Weak	Fort/Forte
Ugly	Mouillé/Mouillée
Difficult	Sec/sèche
Beautiful	Difficile

Translate: By memory only first, then fill in any missing words with help from the previous page.

Dry	Stupid	Ugly
Wet	Easy	Slow
Difficult	Smart	Weak
Beautiful	Strong	Fast

Mignon/Mignonne

mee.ny**oh**/mee.nyon   Cute

Intéressant/Intéressante

uh.teh.reh.s**ah**/**ah**t Interesting

Drôle

drohl   Funny

Différent/Différente

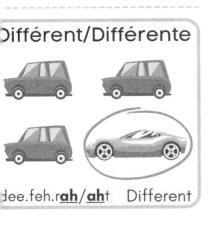

dee.feh.r**ah**/**ah**t   Different

Similaire

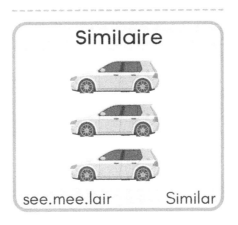

see.mee.lair   Similar

Tôt

toh   Early

Tard

tahr   Late

Long/Longue

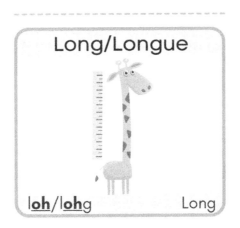

l**oh**/l**oh**g   Long

Court/Courte

koor/koort   Short

Gratuit

grah.tüee   Free

Cher/Chère

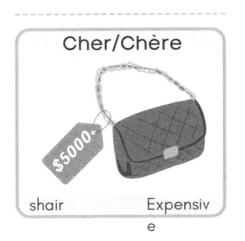

shair   Expensive

Pas cher/Pas chère

pah shair   Cheap/Inexpensive

Expensive •	Drôle
Long •	Pas cher/ Pas chère
Different •	Tôt
Cheap/ Inexpensive •	Cher/Chère
Interesting •	Mignon/ Mignonne
Early •	Gratuit
Late •	Long/Longue
Short •	Similaire
Cute •	Intéressant/ Intéressante
Funny •	Court/Courte
Similar •	Différent/ Différente
Free •	Tard

Translate: By memory only first, then fill in any missing words with help from the previous page.

Similar	Free	Different
The	Long	Interesting
Late	Cheap/Inexpensive	Early
Expensive	Funny	Short

Les adjectifs (4) - Adjectives (4) (Masc./Fem.)

Riche

eesh — Rich

Pauvre

pohvr — Poor

Stressant/Stressante

streh.**sah**/streh.**sah**t — Stressful

Agréable

ah.greh.ahbl — Pleasant

Délicieux/Délicieuse

deh.lee.syuh/syuhz — Delicious

Dégoutant/Dégoutante

deh.goo.**tah**/t**ah**t — Disgusting

Stricte

streekt — Strict

Chaud/Chaude

shoh/shohd — Hot

Froid/Froide

frwah/frwahd — Cold

Bon/Bonne

b**oh**/bonn — Good

Mauvais/Mauvaise

moh.vay/moh.vayz — Bad

Nouveau/Nouvelle

noo.voh/noo.vel — New

▶ **Connect each English word to its correct translation:**

Delicious	•	Délicieux/Délicieuse
New	•	Froid/Froide
Rich	•	Agréable
Good	•	Stricte
Stressful	•	Mauvais/Mauvaise
Strict	•	Pauvre
Hot	•	Stressant/Stressante
Pleasant	•	Riche
Bad	•	Dégoutant/Dégoutante
Cold	•	Bon/Bonne
Poor	•	Chaud/Chaude
Disgusting	•	Nouveau/Nouvelle

(!) **New** (+ masc. noun): "nouvel" before a vowel or H (ex: nouvel **a**mi)

⊖ **Translate:** By memory only first, then fill in any missing words with help from the previous page.

New	Delicious	Good
Stressful	Cold	Strict
Hot	Pleasant	Rich
Poor	Disgusting	Bad

Les animaux (1) - The animals (1)

L'animal (m.)

ah.nee.mahl   animal

Le chat

shah   cat

Le chien

shy**uh**   dog

Le poisson

pwah.s**oh**   fish

Le lapin

lah.p**uh**   bunny

L'oiseau (m.)

wah.zoh   bird

La tortue

tor.tü   turtle

La souris

soo.ree   mouse

Le cheval

shuh.vahl   horse

La vache

vash   cow

Le mouton

moo.t**oh**   sheep

L'âne (m.)

ahn   donkey

Connect each English word to its correct translation:

The turtle	•	Le chien
The bunny	•	La tortue
The horse	•	Le cheval
The cat	•	Le poisson
The donkey	•	Le mouton
The dog	•	L'écureuil
The sheep	•	L'âne
The mouse	•	Le chat
The fish	•	La vache
The cow	•	La souris
The animal	•	Le lapin
The bird	•	L'oiseau

(!) The animal**s** : les anim**aux** (leh zah.nee.moh)

Translate: By memory only first, then fill in any missing words with help from the previous page.

The fish	The turtle	The donkey
The horse	The animal	The cow
The dog	The sheep	The mouse
The bird	The bunny	The cat

Les animaux (2) - The animals (2)

Le lion

ly**oh**   lion

Le tigre

teegr   tiger

L'éléphant (m.)

eh.leh.f**ah**   elephant

La girafe

jee.rahf   giraffe

Le singe

s**uh**j   monkey

Le zèbre

zaybr   zebra

Le loup

loo   wolf

Le crocodile

kroh.koh.deel   crocodile

L'ours

oors   bear

Le rhinocéros

ree.noh.seh.ros   rhinoceros

L'hippopotame

ee.poh.poh.tam   hippo-potamus

L'écureuil

eh.kü.ruh.yuh   squirrel

► **Connect each English word to its correct translation:**

The rhinoceros •	Le rhinocéros
The giraffe •	L'ours
The zebra •	Le tigre
The tiger •	Le crocodile
The bear •	Le zèbre
The elephant •	Le singe
The crocodile •	L'hippopotame
The hippopotamus •	Le loup
The lion •	Le lion
The squirrel •	L'éléphant
The monkey •	La girafe
The wolf •	L'écureuil

→ **Translate:** By memory only first, then fill in any missing words with help from the previous page.

The bear	The tiger	The squirrel
_____	_____	_____
The monkey	The giraffe	The hippopotamus
_____	_____	_____
The lion	The rhinoceros	The zebra
_____	_____	_____
The wolf	The elephant	The crocodile
_____	_____	_____

anslate all the words your remember, check your answers with the word list in p.

.To clean	•	1.To wait	•
.To download	•	2.To scream	•
.To laugh	•	3.To travel	•
.To wash	•	4.To sell	•
.To listen	•	5.To go up	•
.To find	•	6.To answer	•
.To hear	•	7.To finish	•
.To charge	•	8.To start	•
.To stop	•	9.To live	•
.To dance	•	10.Big/Fat	•
.To cry	•	11.Dirty	•
.To sing	•	12.Friendly	•
.To break	•	13.Nice/Kind	•
.To dream	•	14.Young	•
.To choose	•	15.Big/Tall	•
.To play	•	16.Old	•
.To prepare	•	17.Fun	•
.To repair	•	18.Small	•
.To ask	•	19.Clean	•
.To believe	•	20.Mean	•
.To have to/ Must	•	21.Boring	•
.To cut	•	22.Slow	•
.To swim	•	23.Strong	•
.To fall	•	24.Dry	•
.To call	•	25.Easy	•
.To go down	•	26.Wet	•
.To be able to/ Can	•	27.Smart	•

ords to review:

Translate all the words your remember, check your answers with the word list in p.

1. Ugly •	1. Cold •
2. Difficult •	2. Poor •
3. Stupid •	3. Disgusting •
4. Fast •	4. The cat •
5. Weak •	5. The cow •
6. Beautiful •	6. The animal •
7. Funny •	7. The donkey •
8. Similar •	8. The sheep •
9. Interesting •	9. The mouse •
10. Late •	10. The dog •
11. Short •	11. The fish •
12. Early •	12. The bird •
13. Cute •	13. The horse •
14. Free •	14. The bunny •
15. Different •	15. The turtle •
16. Long •	16. The tiger •
17. Expensive •	17. The squirrel •
18. Good •	18. The monkey •
19. Stressful •	19. The bear •
20. Hot •	20. The crocodile •
21. Pleasant •	21. The hippopotamus •
22. Strict •	22. The elephant •
23. Bad •	23. The lion •
24. Rich •	24. The bird •
25. New •	25. The zebra •
26. Delicious •	26. The giraffe •
27. Cheap/ •	27. The rhinoceros •
Inexpensive	

Words to review:

Les oiseaux - The birds

La chauve-souris

shohv.soo.ree   bat

Le hibou

ee.boo   owl

L'autruche (f.)

oh.trüsh   ostrich

La dinde

d**uh**nd   turkey

Le canard

kah.nahr   duck

L'oie (f.)

wah   goose

L'aigle (m.)

aygl   eagle

Le corbeau

kor.boh   crow

Le flamant rose

flah.m**ah**   flamingo

Le perroquet

peh.roh.keh   parrot

Le pingouin

p**uh**.gw**uh**   penguin

Le poulet

poo.lay   chicken

Connect each English word to its correct translation:

The eagle •	Le canard
The penguin •	Le hibou
The duck •	Le flamant rose
The bat •	L'oie
The ostrich •	Le pingouin
The flamingo •	L'autruche
The owl •	Le poulet
The parrot •	L'aigle
The goose •	La chauve-souris
The turkey •	Le perroquet
The crow •	La dinde
The chicken •	Le corbeau

Translate: By memory only first, then fill in any missing words with help from the previous page.

The flamingo	The parrot	The chicken
The owl	The ostrich	The goose
The crow	The eagle	The turkey
The duck	The bat	The penguin

Les insectes et reptiles - Insects and reptiles

Le serpent

sair.p**ah**   snake

Le lézard

leh.zahr   lizard

La grenouille

gruh.noo.yuh   frog

Le scorpion

skor.py**oh**   scorpion

L'araignée (f.)

ah.reh.nyeh   spider

L'insecte (m.)
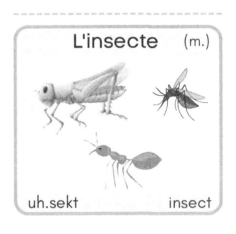
uh.sekt   insect

L'abeille (f.)

ah.bay   bee

Le papillon

pah.pee.y**oh**   butterfly

La mouche

moosh   fly

Le moustique

moos.teek   mosquito

La fourmi

foor.mee   ant

Le cafard

kah.far   cockroach

➤ **Connect each English word to its correct translation:**

The scorpion •	La grenouille
The bee •	Le lézard
The snake •	La mouche
The spider •	L'abeille
The ant •	Le cafard
The lizard •	L'araignée
The mosquito •	Le moustique
The fly •	Le serpent
The frog •	La fourmi
The butterfly •	Le scorpion
The insect •	Le papillon
The cockroach •	L'insecte

➡ **Translate:** By memory only first, then fill in any missing words with help from the previous page.

The bee	The ant	The butterfly
The fly	The scorpion	The spider
The snake	The insect	The cockroach
The frog	The mosquito	The lizard

Les animaux marins - Sea animals

La baleine

bah.layn   whale

Le dauphin

doh.**fuh**   fac   dolphin

Le requin

ruh.**kuh**   shark

L'orque   (f.)

ork   orca/ killer whale

La pieuvre

pyuhvr   octopus

Le calamar

kah.lah.mahr   squid

La méduse
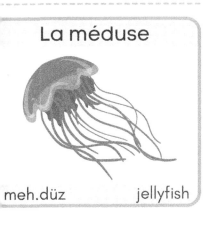
meh.düz   jellyfish

Le homard

oh.mahr   lobster

Le thon

t**oh**   tuna

L'huître   (f.)
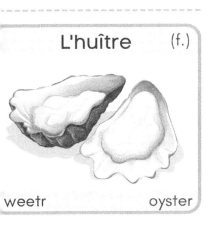
weetr   oyster

Le phoque

fok   seal

L'anguille   (f.)

ah.ghee   eel

> **Connect each English word to its correct translation:**

The orca (killer whale)	La méduse
The jellyfish	La baleine
The shark	L'huître
The dolphin	L'orque
The oyster	Le phoque
The lobster	Le thon
The seal	L'anguille
The squid	Le dauphin
The octopus	Le homard
The tuna	La pieuvre
The eel	Le requin
The whale	Le calamar

Translate: By memory only first, then fill in any missing words with help from the previous page.

The whale	The oyster	The lobster
The jellyfish	The octopus	The seal
The dolphin	The shark	The eel
The tuna	The squid	The orca/killer whale

Les sports - Sports

Le foot / football

oot/foot.bohl — Soccer

Le football américain

foot.bohl ah.meh.ree.k**uh** — Football

Le basketball (basket)

bass.ket.bohl — Basketball

Le tennis

eh.nees — Tennis

Le baseball

behz.bohl — Baseball

Le volley-ball (volley)

voh.leh bohl — Volleyball

La natation

nah.tah.sy**oh** — Swimming

La gymnastique

jeem.nass.teek — Gymnastics

Le patinage

pah.tee.nahj — Ice skating

La musculation

mü.skü.lah.sy**oh** — Weight training

Le ping-pong

peeng.pong — Ping-pong

Le ski

skee — Skiing

➤ **Connect each English word to its correct translation:**

Skiing	•	Le baseball
Tennis	•	Le basketball
Volleyball	•	Le patinage
Soccer	•	Le ping-pong
Football	•	Le foot / football
Ice skating	•	Le tennis
Baseball	•	Le football américain
Ping-pong	•	La natation
Gymnastics	•	La musculation
Weight training	•	Le volley-ball
Swimming	•	Le ski
Basketball	•	La gymnastique

(!) Also Ping-Pong = Tennis de table (teh.nees duh tahbl)

Translate: By memory only first, then fill in any missing words with help from the previous page.

Volleyball	Ice skating	Ping-pong
Baseball	Weight training	Skiing
Gymnastics	Swimming	Tennis
Football	Soccer	Basketball

178

La musique - Music

Le musicien

mü.zee.sy**uh**   musician

Le concert

k**oh**.sair   concert

La musique

mü.zeek   music

L'instrument

uh.strü.m**ah**   instrument

Le piano

pyah.noh   piano

La guitare

ghee.tahr   guitar

La batterie

bah.tree   drums

Le violon

vyoh.l**oh**   violin

Le saxophone

sak.soh.fon   saxophone

La trompette

tr**oh**.pet   trumpet

Le tambour

t**ah**.boor   drum

La flûte

flüt   flute/recorder

► **Connect each English word to its correct translation:**

The drum •   La trompette

The drums •   La musique

The violin •   Le musicien

The instrument •   La guitare

The guitar •   La batterie

The piano •   L'instrument

The flute/recorder •   Le tambour

The saxophone •   La flûte

The trumpet •   Le piano

The concert •   Le violon

The musician •   Le concert

The music •   Le saxophone

Translate: By memory only first, then fill in any missing words with help from the previous page.

The saxophone	The violin	The musician
The drums	The flute/recorder	The guitar
The drum	The concert	The trumpet
The piano	The instrument	The music

Les outils - Tools

L'outil (m.)
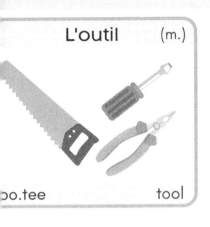
oo.tee   tool

Le marteau

mahr.toh   hammer

La hache

ash   ax

Le tournevis
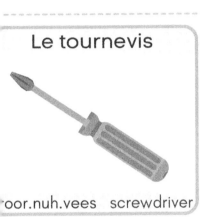
oor.nuh.vees   screwdriver

La scie

see   saw

La règle
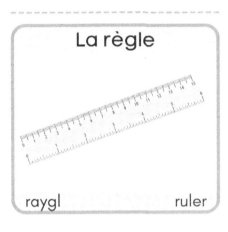
raygl   ruler

Le vis

vees   screw

La perceuse électrique

pair.suhz
eh.lek.treek   power drill

Le scotch

skotsh   (scotch) tape

La corde

kord   rope

L'échelle (f.)

eh.shell   ladder

La pile

peel   battery

► **Connect each English word to its correct translation:**

The ax	L'outil
The rope	La règle
The screwdriver	La perceuse électrique
The ladder	La hache
The saw	La corde
The tool	L'échelle
The power drill	Le tournevis
The battery	Le scotch
The ruler	Le vis
The screw	Le scotch
The (scotch) tape	Le marteau
The hammer	La pile

 Scotch tape aslo: **Le ruban adhésif** (rü.b**ah** ah.deh.zeef)

Translate: By memory only first, then fill in any missing words with help from the previous page.

The saw	The hammer	The screw
The tool	The battery	The (scotch) tape
The rope	The screwdriver	The ladder
The ax	The ruler	The power drill

Les couleurs - The colors (Color the shapes)

La couleur

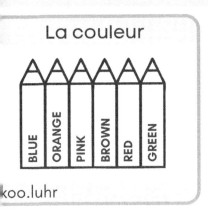

koo.luhr

Bleu

bluh   Blue

Blanc

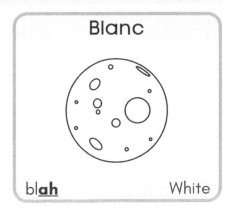

bl**ah**   White

Rouge

rooj   Red

Vert

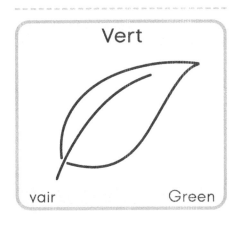

vair   Green

Orange

oh.r**ah**j   Orange

Noir

nwahr   Black

Rose

roz   Pink

Gris

gree   Grey

Violet

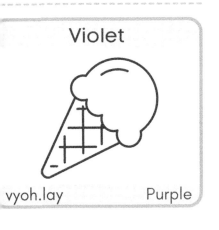

vyoh.lay   Purple

Jaune

joh.n   Yellow

Marron

mah.r**oh**   Brown

➤ Connect each English word to its correct translation:

Black •	Jaune
The color •	Bleu
Purple •	Orange
Yellow •	La couleur
Blue •	Marron
Brown •	Rouge
Red •	Gris
Green •	Noir
White •	Blanc
Grey •	Vert
Pink •	Violet
Orange •	Rose

Translate: By memory only first, then fill in any missing words with help from the previous page.

White	Grey	Yellow
Black	Red	Pink
The color	Brown	Orange
Purple	Blue	Green

Le monde - The world

Le monde

m**oh**nd — world

Le continent

koh.tee.n**ah** — continent

L'océan (m.)
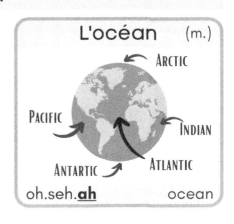
oh.seh.**ah** — ocean

L'Amérique du Nord (f.)
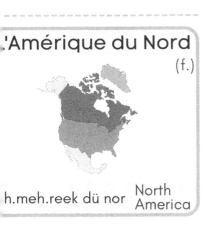
h.meh.reek dü nor — North America

L'Amérique du Sud (f.)

ah.meh.reek dü süd — South America

L'Europe (f.)
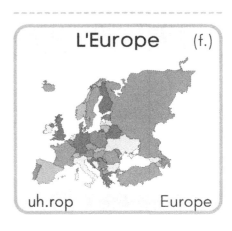
uh.rop — Europe

L'Afrique (f.)
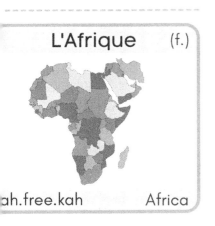
ah.free.kah — Africa

L'Asie (f.)

ah.zee — Asia

L'Océanie (f.)
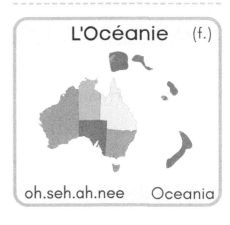
oh.seh.ah.nee — Oceania

L'Antarctique
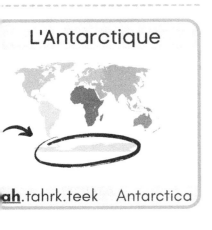
ah.tahrk.teek — Antarctica

L'Arctique
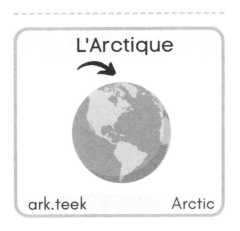
ark.teek — Arctic

Le pays

pay.ee — country

► Connect each English word to its correct translation:

Africa •	L'Amérique du Nord
The world •	Le monde
Oceania •	L'Arctique
The continent •	Le continent
North America •	L'Asie
Europe •	L'océan
The ocean •	L'Amérique du Sud
Asia •	Le pays
Antarctica •	L'Antarctique
South America •	L'Europe
The Arctic •	L'Afrique
The country •	L'Océanie

⊖ Translate: By memory only first, then fill in any missing words with help from the previous page.

South America	Antarctica	North America
The world	The ocean	The Arctic
Asia	Europe	Oceania
The continent	The country	Africa

Les pays - The countries

La France

frahs   France

Les États-Unis (m.)

eh.tah.zü.nee   United States

Le Royaume-Uni

rwah.yohm ü.nee   United Kingdom

L'Espagne (f.)

ess.pah.nyuh   Spain

Le Canada

kah.nah.dah   Canada

L'Italie (f.)

ee.tah.lee   Italy

Le Mexique

meh.kseek   Mexico

L'Allemagne (f.)

ahl.mah.nyuh   Germany

Le Maroc

mah.rok   Morocco

La Chine

sheen   China

Le Japon

jah.poh   Japan

Le Brésil

breh.zeel   Brasil

Connect each English word to its correct translation:

Spain   •   L'Italie

France   •   L'Allemagne

Morocco   •   Le Brésil

Brasil   •   La France

The United States   •   Le Canada

Canada   •   Le Mexique

Mexico   •   Les États-Unis

United Kingdom   •   Le Japon

China   •   Le Maroc

Germany   •   La Chine

Japan   •   L'Espagne

Italy   •   Le Royaume-Uni

Translate: By memory only first, then fill in any missing words with help from the previous page.

Morocco	Italy	The United States
China	Mexico	Germany
England	Spain	Japan
Canada	Brasil	France

anslate all the words your remember, check your answers with the word list in p.

The bat •	1. The dolphin •
The turkey •	2. The tuna •
The crow •	3. The eel •
The ostrich •	4. The oyster •
The owl •	5. The seal •
The parrot •	6. The squid •
The flamingo •	7. The lobster •
The goose •	8. The octopus •
The chicken •	9. The whale •
The duck •	10. Soccer •
The penguin •	11. Weight training •
The eagle •	12. Swimming •
The spider •	13. Football •
The butterfly •	14. Baseball •
The insect •	15. Ping-pong •
The ant •	16. Ice skating •
The mosquito •	17. Gymnastics •
The fly •	18. Basketball •
The lizard •	19. Volleyball •
The frog •	20. Tennis •
The cockroach •	21. Skiing •
The snake •	22. The instrument •
The bee •	23. The guitar •
The scorpion •	24. The piano •
The shark •	25. The violin •
The jellyfish •	26. The drums •
The orca •	27. The drum •
(killer whale)	

ords to review:

Translate all the words your remember, check your answers with the word list in p.

1. The concert •	1. Grey •
2. The musician •	2. Pink •
3. The flute/recorder •	3. Orange •
4. The saxophone •	4. The continent •
5. The trumpet •	5. South America •
6. The music •	6. The Arctic •
7. The ladder •	7. North America •
8. The screw •	8. The ocean •
9. The (scotch) tape •	9. Asia •
10. The saw •	10. Europe •
11. The power drill •	11. Antarctica •
12. The battery •	12. The country •
13. The tool •	13. Oceania •
14. The ruler •	14. The world •
15. The hammer •	15. Africa •
16. The screwdriver •	16. Brasil •
17. The rope •	17. Germany •
18. The ax •	18. Japan •
19. Yellow •	19. The United States •
20. Blue •	20. Mexico •
21. Red •	21. United Kingdom •
22. Green •	22. Canada •
23. Brown •	23. China •
24. White •	24. Italy •
25. Purple •	25. Morocco •
26. The color •	26. France •
27. Black •	27. Spain •

Words to review:

Les nationalités - The nationalities

américain/américain

ah.meh.ree.k**uh**
ah.meh.ree.ken   American

français/français

fr**ah**.say/fr**ah**.sayz   French

anglais/anglaise

ah.glay/**ah**.glayz   English

canadien/canadienne

kah.nah.dy**uh**
kah.nah.dyen   Canadian

espagnol/espagnole

ehs.pah.nyol   Spanish

italien/italienne

ee.tahl.y**uh**
ee.tahl.yen   Italian

mexicain/mexicaine

meh.xee.k**uh**
meh.xee.ken   Mexican

allemand/allemande

ahl.m**ah**/ahl.m**ah**d   German

marocain/marocaine

mah.roh.k**uh**
mah.roh.ken   Moroccan

chinois/chinoise

shee.nwah
shee.nwahz   Chinese

japonais/japonaise

jah.poh.nay
jah.poh.nayz   Japanese

brésilien/brésilienne

breh.zeel.y**uh**
breh.zeel.yen   Brasilian

Mexican •	japonais(e)
Chinese •	anglais(e)
Canadian •	mexicain(e)
Italian •	espagnol(e)
French •	allemand(e)
Spanish •	italien/italienne
English •	français(e)
German •	chinois(e)
American •	canadien/canadienne
Moroccan •	marocain(e)
Brasilian •	américain(e)
Japanese •	brésilien/brésilienne

Translate: By memory only first, then fill in any missing words with help from the previous page.

Canadian	Brasilian	Mexican
Italian	Spanish	Moroccan
Chinese	American	French
English	German	Japanese

L'espace - Space

La planète

olah.net   planet

Le système solaire

sees.tem soh.lair   solar system

L'espace (m.)
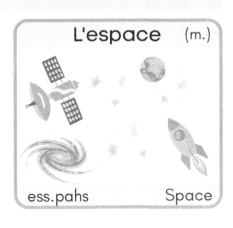
ess.pahs   Space

La lune

ün   moon

Mercure

mair.kür   Mercury

Vénus

veh.nüs   Venus

La terre
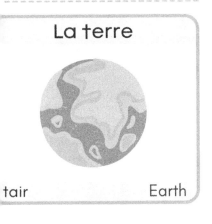
tair   Earth

Mars
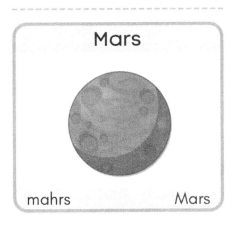
mahrs   Mars

Jupiter

jü.pee.tair   Jupiter

Saturne

sah.türn   Saturn

Uranus
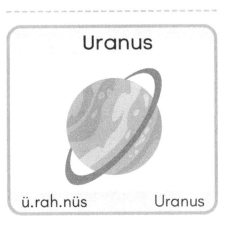
ü.rah.nüs   Uranus

Neptune
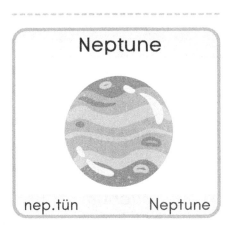
nep.tün   Neptune

► **Connect each English word to its correct translation:**

Saturn •	Mars
The solar system •	Uranus
Jupiter •	La planète
Mars •	Saturne
Neptune •	La terre
Venus •	Jupiter
Earth •	Neptune
The moon •	Mercure
Uranus •	Le système solaire
Mercury •	La lune
The planet •	L'espace
Space •	Vénus

Translate: By memory only first, then fill in any missing words with help from the previous page.

Uranus	The moon	Space
Jupiter	The planet	Earth
Neptune	Mars	Saturn
Venus	The solar system	Mercury

Les formes - Shapes

Le cercle

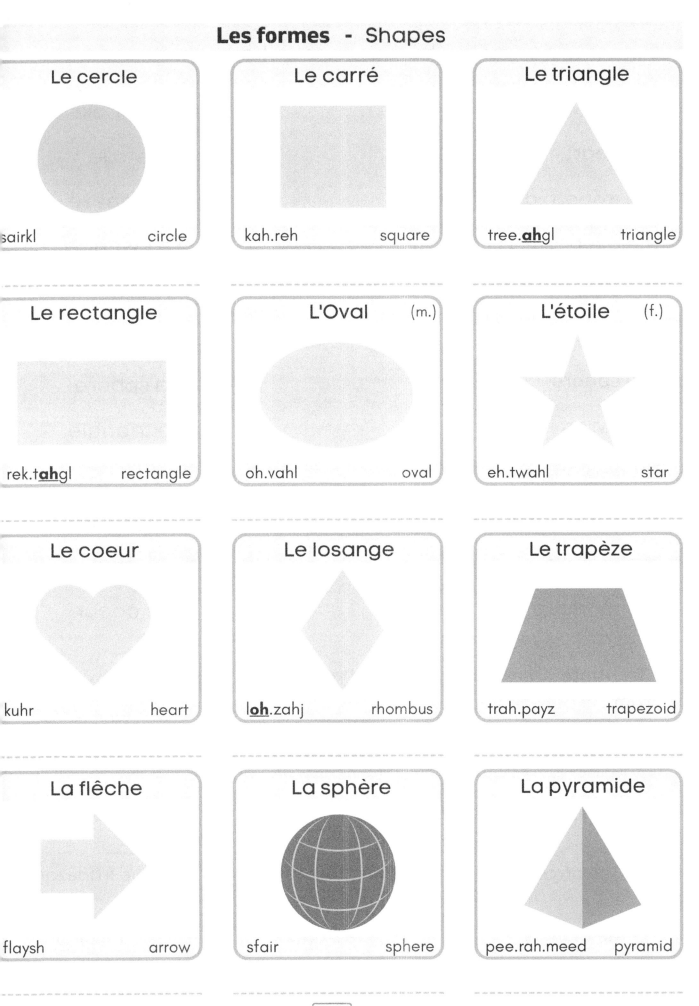

sairkl   circle

Le carré

kah.reh   square

Le triangle

tree.**ah**gl   triangle

Le rectangle

rek.t**ah**gl   rectangle

L'Oval   (m.)

oh.vahl   oval

L'étoile   (f.)

eh.twahl   star

Le coeur

kuhr   heart

Le losange

l**oh**.zahj   rhombus

Le trapèze

trah.payz   trapezoid

La flèche

flaysh   arrow

La sphère

sfair   sphere

La pyramide

pee.rah.meed   pyramid

➤ Connect each English word to its correct translation:

The arrow •		Le cercle
The heart •		L'étoile
The trapezoid •		Le trapèze
The oval •		Le losange
The star •		La pyramide
The square •		Le rectangle
The sphere •		La sphère
The pyramid •		Le triangle
The rectangle •		La flèche
The circle •		Le carré
The triangle •		L'oval
The rhombus •		Le coeur

Translate: By memory only first, then fill in any missing words with help from the previous page.

The heart	The sphere	The pyramid
The oval	The square	The star
The arrow	The rhombus	The trapezoid
The triangle	The rectangle	The circle

Les nombres de 0 à 100 (1) - Numbers from 0 to 100 (1)

Le nombre  nohbr — number	**Zéro** 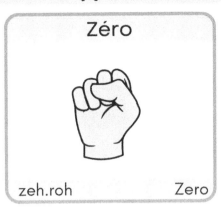 zeh.roh — Zero	**Un**  uh — One
Deux 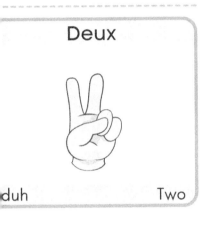 duh — Two	**Trois** 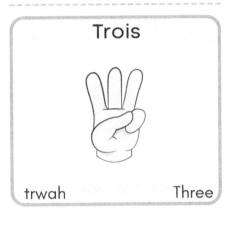 trwah — Three	**Quatre**  kahtr — Four
Cinq 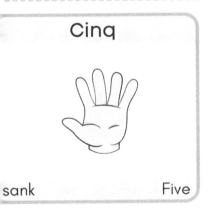 sank — Five	**Six**  sees — Six	**Sept**  set — Seven
Huit  weet — Eight	**Neuf**  nuhf — Nine	**Dix** 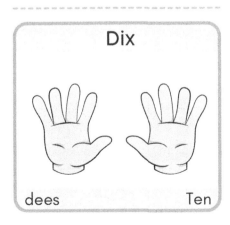 dees — Ten

▶ **Connect each English word to its correct translation:**

Five	•		Huit
The number	•		Trois
Ten	•		Six
Eight	•		Un
Zero	•		Dix
Six	•		Le nombre
One	•		Neuf
Four	•		Quatre
Two	•		Zéro
Nine	•		Sept
Seven	•		Cinq
Three	•		Deux

➔ **Translate:** By memory only first, then fill in any missing words with help from the previous page.

Two	Seven	Zero
_____	_____	_____
Six	Three	Nine
_____	_____	_____
One	The number	Ten
_____	_____	_____
Four	Eight	Five
_____	_____	_____

Onze

ohz   Eleven

Douze

dooz   Twelve

Treize

trayz   Thirteen

Quatorze
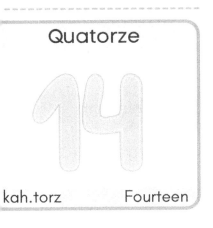
kah.torz   Fourteen

Quinze

k**uh**z   Fifteen

Seize

sayz   Sixteen

Dix-sept

dee.set   Seventeen

Dix-huit

deez.weet   Eighteen

Dix-neuf

deez.nuhf   Nineteen

Vingt

v**uh**   Twenty

Vingt et un

v**uh**.teh.**uh**   Twenty-one

Vingt-deux

v**uh**t.duh   Twenty-two

➤ Connect each English word to its correct translation:

Twenty-one •	Vingt-deux
Fourteen •	Dix-neuf
Twenty •	Onze
Sixteen •	Quinze
Nineteen •	Vingt et un
Twelve •	Douze
Twenty-two •	Dix-sept
Thirteen •	Vingt
Eighteen •	Dix-huit
Fifteen •	Treize
Eleven •	Seize
Seventeen •	Quatorze

Translate: By memory only first, then fill in any missing words with help from the previous page.

Sixteen	Thirteen	Twenty-one
Twelve	Seventeen	Eleven
Fourteen	Eighteen	Twenty-two
Nineteen	Twenty	Fifteen

Vingt-trois

v**uh**t.trwah   Twenty-three

Vingt-quatre

v**uh**t.katr   Twenty-four

Vingt-cinq

v**uh**t.sank   Twenty-five

Vingt-six

v**uh**t.sees   Twenty-six

Vingt-sept

v**uh**t.set   Twenty-seven

Vingt-huit

v**uh**t.weet   Twenty-eight

Vingt-neuf

v**uh**t.nuhf   Twenty-nine

Trente

tr**ah**t   Thirty

Trente et un

tr**ah**t eh **uh**   Thirty-one

Trente-deux

tr**ah**t duh   Thirty-two

Trente-trois

tr**ah**t trwah   Thirty-three

Trente-quatre

tr**ah**t kahtr   Thirty-four

➤ Connect each English word to its correct translation:

Twenty-eight •	Vingt-trois
Thirty-three •	Vingt-neuf
Twenty-six •	Trente-quatre
Thirty-two •	Vingt-six
Twenty-three •	Trente
Thirty •	Vingt-quatre
Thirty-one •	Trente et un
Twenty-four •	Vingt-huit
Thirty-four •	Trente-trois
Twenty-seven •	Vingt-cinq
Twenty-five •	Trente-deux
Twenty-nine •	Vingt-sept

Translate: By memory only first, then fill in any missing words with help from the previous page.

Twenty-three	Thirty	Thirty-one
Twenty-six	Twenty-eight	Thirty-four
Thirty-two	Twenty-five	Thirty-three
Twenty-seven	Twenty-nine	Twenty-four

Trente-cinq

rraht sank — Thirty-five

Trente-six

traht sees — Thirty-six

Trente-sept

traht set — Thirty-seven

Trente-huit

traht weet — Thirty-eight

Trente-neuf

traht nuhf — Thirty-nine

Quarante

kah.raht — Forty

Quarante et un

kah.raht.eh.uh — Forty-one

Quarante-deux

kah.raht.duh — Forty-two

Quarante-trois

kah.raht.trwah — Forty-three

Quarante-quatre

kah.raht.kahtr — Forty-four

Quarante-cinq

kah.raht.sank — Forty-five

Quarante-six

kah.raht.sees — Forty-six

Forty •	Trente-neuf
Forty-two •	Trente-sept
Thirty-eight •	Quarante-deux
Forty-three •	Quarante-six
Thirty-six •	Trente-huit
Forty-six •	Quarante-cinq
Thirty-seven •	Quarante-trois
Forty-five •	Quarante
Forty-one •	Quarante et un
Thirty-nine •	Trente-cinq
Forty-four •	Quarante-quatre
Thirty-five •	Trente-six

⊙ **Translate:** By memory only first, then fill in any missing words with help from the previous page.

Forty	Thirty-six	Forty-three
Thirty-eight	Forty-two	Forty-six
Forty-four	Forty-one	Thirty-seven
Thirty-five	Forty-five	Thirty-nine

Quarante-sept

ah.**rah**t.set   Forty-seven

Quarante-huit

kah.**rah**t.weet   Forty-eight

Quarante-neuf

kah.**rah**t.nuhf   Forty-nine

Cinquante

suh.**kah**t   Fifty

Cinquante et un

suh.**kah**t.eh.**uh**   Fifty-one

Cinquante-deux

suh.**kah**t.duh   Fifty-two

Cinquante-trois

suh.**kah**t.trwah   Fifty-three

Cinquante-quatre

suh.**kah**t.kahtr   Fifty-four

Cinquante-cinq

suh.**kah**t.sank   Fifty-five

Cinquante-six

suh.**kah**t.sees   Fifty-six

Cinquante-sept

s**uh**.**kah**t.set   Fifty-seven

Cinquante-huit

suh.**kah**t.weet   Fifty-eight

Forty-seven •	Quarante-huit
Fifty •	Cinquante et un
Fifty-seven •	Cinquante-quatre
Fifty-two •	Cinquante-sept
Forty-nine •	Cinquante-six
Fifty-three •	Cinquante-huit
Fifty-six •	Cinquante-trois
Fifty-one •	Quarante-neuf
Fifty-four •	Cinquante-deux
Forty-eight •	Quarante-sept
Fifty-five •	Cinquante
Fifty-eight •	Cinquante-cinq

→ **Translate:** By memory only first, then fill in any missing words with help from the previous page.

Fifty-two	Fifty-five	Fifty-eight
Fifty-seven	Forty-seven	Fifty
Fifty-four	Fifty-one	Fifty-three
Fifty-six	Forty-nine	Forty-eight

Cinquante-neuf

uh.kaht.nuhf   Fifty-nine

Soixante

swah.saht   Sixty

Soixante et un

swah.saht.eh.uh   Sixty-one

Soixante-deux

swat.saht.duh   Sixty-two

Soixante-trois

swah.saht.trwah   Sixty-three

Soixante-quatre

swah.saht.kahtr   Sixty-four

Soixante-cinq

swah.saht.sank   Sixty-five

Soixante-six

swah.saht.sees   Sixty-six

Soixante-sept

swah.saht.set   Sixty-seven

Soixante-huit

swah.saht.weet   Sixty-eight

Soixante-neuf

swah.saht.weet   Sixty-nine

Soixante-dix

swah.saht.dees   Seventy

Sixty-eight •	Soixante-neuf
Sixty-nine •	Soixante
Seventy •	Soixante-trois
Fifty-nine •	Cinquante-neuf
Sixty •	Soixante-cinq
Sixty-one •	Soixante-dix
Sixty-two •	Soixante-sept
Sixty-three •	Soixante-six
Sixty-four •	Soixante-huit
Sixty-five •	Soixante-quatre
Sixty-six •	Soixante et un
Sixty-seven •	Soixante-deux

Translate: By memory only first, then fill in any missing words with help from the previous page.

Fifty-nine	Sixty-nine	Sixty
Sixty-three	Sixty-two	Sixty-five
Sixty-eight	Sixty-six	Sixty-seven
Sixty-one	Seventy	Sixty-four

anslate all the words your remember, check your answers with the word list in p.

Italian (f.)	•	1. The oval	•
Moroccan (m.)	•	2. The circle	•
Brasilian (f.)	•	3. The triangle	•
French (f.)	•	4. The star	•
English (m.)	•	5. The sphere	•
German (f.)	•	6. The pyramid	•
Spanish (m.)	•	7. The square	•
American (f.)	•	8. The rectangle	•
Japanese (m.)	•	9. The rhombus	•
Canadian (f.)	•	10. Eight	•
Chinese (m.)	•	11. Nine	•
Mexican (m.)	•	12. Seven	•
Mars	•	13. Zero	•
Mercury	•	14. One	•
The planet	•	15. Four	•
Neptune	•	16. Six	•
Earth	•	17. Two	•
The moon	•	18. Three	•
Venus	•	19. Ten	•
Uranus	•	20. The number	•
Space	•	21. Five	•
Jupiter	•	22. Sixteen	•
The solar system	•	23. Nineteen	•
Saturn	•	24. Twelve	•
The trapezoid	•	25. Twenty	•
The heart	•	26. Fourteen	•
The arrow	•	27. Twenty-one	•

'ords to review:

Translate all the numbers your remember, check your answers with the word list in p.

A	B
1. Fifteen •	1. Thirty-nine •
2. Eleven •	2. Forty-four •
3. Twenty-two •	3. Thirty-five •
4. Thirteen •	4. Fifty-two •
5. Eighteen •	5. Forty-eight •
6. Seventeen •	6. Fifty-five •
7. Thirty-two •	7. Forty-nine •
8. Twenty-seven •	8. Fifty-six •
9. Twenty-five •	9. Fifty-one •
10. Twenty-three •	10. Fifty-three •
11. Thirty-one •	11. Fifty-four •
12. Twenty-four •	12. Fifty-eight •
13. Thirty •	13. Fifty-seven •
14. Thirty-four •	14. Fifty •
15. Twenty-nine •	15. Forty-seven •
16. Twenty-six •	16. Fifty-nine •
17. Thirty-three •	17. Sixty-five •
18. Twenty-eight •	18. Sixty-six •
19. Forty-three •	19. Sixty •
20. Thirty-six •	20. Sixty-two •
21. Thirty-seven •	21. Sixty-three •
22. Forty-five •	22. Sixty-one •
23. Forty-six •	23. Sixty-four •
24. Forty-one •	24. Sixty-seven •
25. Thirty-eight •	25. Seventy •
26. Forty-two •	26. Sixty-nine •
27. Forty •	27. Sixty-eight •

Words to review:

Soixante et onze

wah.s**ah**t.eh.**oh**z Seventy-one

Soixante-douze

swah.s**ah**t.dooz Seventy-two

Soixante-treize

swah.s**ah**t.trayz Seventy-three

Soixante-quatorze

wah.s**ah**t.kah.torz Seventy-four

Soixante-quinze

swah.s**ah**t.kah.torz Seventy-five

Soixante-seize

swah.s**ah**t.sayz Seventy-six

Soixante-dix-sept

wah.s**ah**t.dees.set Seventy-seven

Soixante-dix-huit

swah.s**ah**t.dees.weet Seventy-eight

Soixante-dix-neuf

swah.s**ah**t.dees.nuhf Seventy-nine

Quatre-vingt<u>s</u>
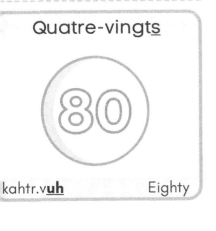
kahtr.v**uh** Eighty

Quatre-vingt-un

kahtr.v**uh**.**uh** Eighty-one

Quatre-vingt-deux

kahtr.v**uh**.duh Eighty-two

▶ **Connect each English word to its correct translation:**

Seventy-five •	Soixante-treize
Eighty •	Soixante-seize
Seventy-six •	Quatre-vingt-deux
Seventy-two •	Soixante-dix-sept
Seventy-four •	Soixante-dix-neuf
Seventy-eight •	Soixante et onze
Seventy-one •	Soixante-dix-huit
Seventy-three •	Soixante-quatorze
Seventy-seven •	Soixante-quinze
Eighty-one •	Quatre-vingts
Eighty-two •	Soixante-douze
Seventy-nine •	Quatre-vingt-un

Translate: By memory only first, then fill in any missing words with help from the previous page.

Seventy-seven	Seventy-one	Seventy-six
Seventy-nine	Seventy-two	Eighty-one
Seventy-three	Eighty-two	Eighty
Seventy-five	Seventy-four	Seventy-eight

Quatre-vingt-trois

ahtr.v**uh**.trwah   Eighty-three

Quatre-vingt-quatre

kahtr.v**uh**.kahtr   Eighty-four

Quatre-vingt-cinq

kahtr.v**uh**.sank   Eighty-five

Quatre-vingt-six

ahtr.v**uh**.sees   Eighty-six

Quatre-vingt-sept

kahtr.v**uh**.set   Eighty-seven

Quatre-vingt-huit

kahtr.v**uh**.weet   Eighty-eight

Quatre-vingt-neuf

kahtr.v**uh**.nuhf   Eighty-nine

Quatre-vingt-dix

kahtr.v**uh**.dees   Ninety

Quatre-vingt-onze

kahtr.v**uh**.**oh**z   Ninety-one

Quatre-vingt-douze

kahtr.v**uh**.dooz   Ninety-two

Quatre-vingt-treize

kahtr.v**uh**.trayz   Ninety-three

Quatre-vingt-quatorze

kahtr.v**uh**.kah.torz   Ninety-four

► Connect each English word to its correct translation:

Eighty-five •	Quatre-vingt-trois
Eighty-three •	Quatre-vingt-six
Eighty-six •	Quatre-vingt-neuf
Eighty-four •	Quatre-vingt-huit
Ninety-one •	Quatre-vingt-quatre
Eighty-eight •	Quatre-vingt-onze
Ninety-two •	Quatre-vingt-douze
Ninety •	Quatre-vingt-cinq
Ninety-three •	Quatre-vingt-quatorze
Eighty-seven •	Quatre-vingt-dix
Eighty-nine •	Quatre-vingt-sept
Ninety-four •	Quatre-vingt-treize

Translate: By memory only first, then fill in any missing words with help from the previous page.

Eighty-five	Eighty-seven	Eighty-eight
Eighty-six	Ninety-two	Ninety
Eighty-one	Eighty-three	Ninety-one
Eighty-two	Eighty-nine	Eighty-four

Quatre-vingt-quinze

kahtr.**vuh**.ku**hz**   Ninety-five

Quatre-vingt-seize

kahtr.**vuh**.sayz   Ninety-six

Quatre-vingt-dix-sept

kahtr.**vuh**.dee.set   Ninety-seven

Quatre-vingt-dix-huit

ahtr.**vuh**.deez.weet   Ninety-eight

Quatre-vingt-dix-neuf

kahtr.**vuh**.deez.nuhf   Ninety-nine

Cent

s**ah**   One hundred

Cent un

s**ah**.**uh**   One hundred one

Cent deux

s**ah**.duh   One hundred two

Cent trois...

s**ah**.trwah   One hundred three

Deux cent<u>s</u>

duh s**ah**   Two hundred

Deux cent vingt

duh s**ah** v**uh**   Two hundred twenty

Cinq cent un

s**uh** s**ah** **uh**   Five hundred and one

➤ Connect each English word to its correct translation:

Ninety-five	Quatre-vingt-seize
Ninety-six	Deux cent vingt
Ninety-seven	Quatre-vingt-dix-neuf
Ninety-eight	Cent un
Ninety-nine	Cinq cent un
One hundred	Quatre-vingt-dix-sept
One hundred one	Cent
One hundred two	Deux cents
One hundred three	Cent deux
Two hundred	Quatre-vingt-quinze
Ninety-three	Quatre-vingt-dix-huit
Ninety-four	Cent trois...

Translate: By memory only first, then fill in any missing words with help from the previous page.

One hundred three	One hundred	One hundred two
One hundred one	Ninety-six	Two hundred twenty
Ninety-five	Five hundred and one	Two hundred
Ninety-nine	Ninety-eight	Ninety-seven

Les nombres (10) - Numbers (10)

Six cent trente-sept

637

see.sah raht.set — Six hundred thirty seven

Sept cent huit

708

set sah weet — Seven hundred eight

Neuf cent quatre-vingt-dix-neuf

999

nuhf sah kahtr. vuh.deez.nuhf — Nine hundred and ninety nine

Neuf cent onze

911

nuhf sah deez nuhf — Nine hundred eleven

Mille

1000

meel — One thousand

Deux mille vingt-trois

2023

duh meel vaht trwah — Two thousand twenty three

Sept mille six cents

7600

set meel see sah — Seven thousand six hundred

Dix mille

10000

dee meel — Ten thousand

Cinquante mille

50000

suh.kaht meel — fifty thousand

Cent mille

100000

sah meel — One hundred thousand

Un million

1000000

uh mee.lyoh — One million

Un milliard

1000000000

uh mee.lyahr — One billion

► Connect each English word to its correct translation:

Six hundred thirty-seven	Sept cent huit
Seven hundred eight	Deux mille vingt-trois
Nine hundred and ninety-nine	Cent mille
Nine hundred eleven	Neuf cent onze
One thousand	Dix mille
Two thousand twenty-three	Cinquante mille
Seven thousand six hundred	Six cent trente-sept
Ten thousand	Un milliard
Fifty thousand	Mille
One hundred thousand	Neuf cent quatre-vingt-dix-neuf
One million	Un million
One billion	Sept mille six cents

Translate: By memory only first!

(!) **Cent** in the plural (deux cent**s**...) takes an **s** except if followed by other numbers

One thousand	One hundred thousand	One million
Ten thousand	One billion	Seven hundred eigh
Fifty thousand	Nine hundred eleven	Nine hundred and ninety nine
7600	2023	Six hundred thirty seve

anslate all the numbers your remember, check your answers with the word list in p.

71 •	1. **99** •
72 •	2. **100** •
73 •	3. **103** •
74 •	4. **101** •
75 •	5. **102** •
76 •	6. **200** •
77 •	7. **220** •
78 •	8. **205** •
80 •	9. **637** •
81 •	10. **708** •
82 •	11. **999** •
83 •	12. **1000** •
84 •	13. **2023** •
85 •	14. **2024** •
86 •	15. **7,600** •
87 •	16. **10,000** •
88 •	17. **50,000** •
89 •	18. **100,000** •
90 •	19. **1,000,000** •
91 •	20. **1,000,000,000** •
94 •	
97 •	
92 •	
95 •	
96 •	
93 •	
98 •	

Bravo!

ords to review:

ongratulations for completing you vocabulary workbook! We hope you found it to be a great
ool to add to your language learning routine and that you feel confident using your new
ords in conversations in French.

o your best to use this vocabulary regularly so as not to forget it.

emember: *"Words you don't use are words you'll forget!"*

**you enjoyed this book and would like to let us and other language learners know how
ou liked it, we would greatly appreciate a quick review on Amazon!**
means a lot to us!

e wish you great success on your language learning journey!

Merci beaucoup!

The Bilingoal Team!

- -

Want to learn more? Check out our other language learning books an Amazon!

Beginner French Phrases	Beginner French Workbook	Beginner Spanish Workbook

A colorful picture book filled with vocabulary and useful sentences. Great for kids, teens and visual learners in general.	*A fun workbook for beginners to learn new vocabulary and use it to build sentences in French.*	*Same great book... in Spanish!*

- 20 Important Irregular verbs -

Here are 20 highly used irregular verbs in the most commonly used tenses:

PRESENT	PASSÉ COMPOSÉ	IMPARFAIT	FUTUR

To be: ÊTRE

PRESENT	PASSÉ COMPOSÉ	IMPARFAIT	FUTUR
Je **suis**	J'ai **été**	J'**étais**	Je **serai**
Tu **es**	Tu **as été**	Tu **étais**	Tu **seras**
Il / Elle / On **est**	Il / Elle / On **a été**	Il / Elle / On **était**	Il / Elle / On **sera**
Nous **sommes**	Nous **avons été**	Nous **étions**	Nous **serons**
Vous **êtes**	Vous **avez été**	Vous **étiez**	Vous **serez**
Ils / Elles **sont**	Ils / Elles **ont été**	Ils / Elles **étaient**	Ils / Elles **seront**

To Have: AVOIR

PRESENT	PASSÉ COMPOSÉ	IMPARFAIT	FUTUR
J'**ai**	J'ai **eu**	Je **avais**	J'**aurai**
Tu **as**	Tu **as eu**	Tu **avais**	Tu **auras**
Il / Elle / On **a**	Il / Elle / On **a eu**	Il / Elle / On **avait**	Il / Elle / On **aura**
Nous **avons**	Nous **avez eu**	Nous **avions**	Nous **aurons**
Vous **avez**	Vous **ont eu**	Vous **aviez**	Vous **aurez**
Ils / Elles **ont**	Ils / Elles **ont eu**	Ils / Elles **avaient**	Ils / Elles **auront**

TO GO: ALLER

PRESENT	PASSÉ COMPOSÉ	IMPARFAIT	FUTUR
Je **vais**	Je **suis allé (e)** *	J'**allais**	J'**irai**
Tu **vas**	Tu **es allé (e)**	Tu **allais**	Tu **iras**
Il / Elle / On **va**	Il / Elle / On **est allé (e)**	Il / Elle / On **allait**	Il / Elle / On **ira**
Nous **allons**	Nous **sommes allé (e/s)**	Nous **allions**	Nous **irons**
Vous **allez**	Vous **êtes allé (e/s)**	Vous **alliez**	Vous **irez**
Ils / Elles **vont**	Ils / Elles **sont allé (e/s)**	Ils / Elles **allaient**	Ils / Elles **iront**

TO DO: FAIRE

PRESENT	PASSÉ COMPOSÉ	IMPARFAIT	FUTUR
Je **fais**	J'ai **fait**	Je **faisais**	Je **ferai**
Tu **fais**	Tu **as fait**	Tu **faisais**	Tu **feras**
Il / Elle / On **fait**	Il / Elle / On **a fait**	Il / Elle / On **faisait**	Il / Elle / On **fera**
Nous **faisons**	Nous **avez fait**	Nous **faisions**	Nous **ferons**
Vous **faisez**	Vous **avez fait**	Vous **faisiez**	Vous **ferez**
Ils / Elles **font**	Ils / Elles **ont fait**	Ils / Elles **faisaient**	Ils / Elles **feront**

To say: DIRE

PRESENT	PASSÉ COMPOSÉ	IMPARFAIT	FUTUR
Je **dis**	J'ai **dit**	Je **disais**	Je **dirai**
Tu **dis**	Tu **as dit**	Tu **disais**	Tu **diras**
Il / Elle / On **dit**	Il / Elle / On **a dit**	Il / Elle / On **disait**	Il / Elle / On **dira**
Nous **disons**	Nous **avons dit**	Nous **disions**	Nous **dirons**
Vous **disez**	Vous **avez dit**	Vous **disiez**	Vous **direz**
Ils / Elles **disent**	Ils / Elles **ont dit**	Ils / Elles **disaient**	Ils / Elles **diront**

*add -**e** for female and -**s** for plu

BE ABLE TO: POUVOIR

PRESENT	PASSÉ COMPOSÉ	IMPARFAIT	FUTUR
e peux	J'ai pu	Je pouvais	Je pourrai
u peux	Tu as pu	Tu pouvais	Tu pourras
/ Elle / On peut	Il / Elle / On a pu	Il / Elle / On pouvait	Il / Elle / On pourra
ous pouvons	Nous avons pu	Nous pouvions	Nous pourrons
ous pouvez	Vous avez pu	Vous pouviez	Vous pourrez
s / Elles peuvent	Ils / Elles ont pu	Ils / Elles pouvaient	Ils / Elles pourront

want: VOULOIR

PRESENT	PASSÉ COMPOSÉ	IMPARFAIT	FUTUR
veux	J'ai voulu	Je voulais	Je voudrai
veux	Tu as voulu	Tu voulais	Tu voudras
/ Elle / On veut	Il / Elle / On a voulu	Il / Elle / On voulait	Il / Elle / On voudra
ous voulons	Nous avez voulu	Nous voulions	Nous voudrons
ous voulez	Vous ont voulu	Vous vouliez	Vous voudrez
s / Elles veulent	Ils / Elles ont voulu	Ils / Elles avaient	Ils / Elles voudront

know: SAVOIR   (a fact, how to do something...)

PRESENT	PASSÉ COMPOSÉ	IMPARFAIT	FUTUR
e sais	J'ai su	Je savais	Je saurai
u sais	Tu as su	Tu savais	Tu sauras
/ Elle / On sait	Il / Elle / On a su	Il / Elle / On savait	Il / Elle / On saura
ous savons	Nous avons su	Nous savions	Nous saurons
ous savez	Vous avez su	Vous saviez	Vous saurez
s / Elles savent	Ils / Elles ont su	Ils / Elles savaient	Ils / Elles sauront

know: CONNAÎTRE   (someone, a story, a song, a place, an area of study...)

PRESENT	PASSÉ COMPOSÉ	IMPARFAIT	FUTUR
e connais	J'ai connu	Je connaissais	Je connaîtrai
u connais	Tu as connu	Tu connaissais	Tu connaîtras
/ Elle / On connait	Il / Elle / On a connu	Il / Elle / On connaissait	Il / Elle / On connaîtra
ous connaissons	Nous avez connu	Nous connaissions	Nous connaîtrons
ous connaissez	Vous avez connu	Vous connaissiez	Vous connaîtrez
s / Elles connaissent	Ils / Elles ont connu	Ils / Elles connaissaient	Ils / Elles connaîtront

to have to/ Must: DEVOIR

PRESENT	PASSÉ COMPOSÉ	IMPARFAIT	FUTUR
e dois	J'ai dû	Je devais	Je devrais
u dois	Tu as dû	Tu devais	Tu devras
/ Elle / On doit	Il / Elle / On a dû	Il / Elle / On devait	Il / Elle / On devra
ous devons	Nous avons dû	Nous devions	Nous devrons
ous devez	Vous avez dû	Vous deviez	Vous devrez
s / Elles doivent	Ils / Elles ont dû	Ils / Elles devaient	Ils / Elles devront

PRESENT	PASSÉ COMPOSÉ	IMPARFAIT	FUTUR

To learn: APPRENDRE

J'apprends	J'ai appris	J'apprenais	j'apprendrai
Tu apprends	Tu as appris	Tu apprenais	Tu apprendras
Il / Elle / On apprends	Il / Elle / On a appris	Il / Elle / On apprenait	Il /Elle / On apprendr
Nous apprenons	Nous avons appris	Nous apprenions	Nous apprendrons
Vous apprenez	Vous avez appris	Vous appreniez	Vous apprendrez
Ils / Elles apprennent	Ils / Elles ont appris	Ils / Elles apprennent	Ils/Elles apprendront

To take: PRENDRE

Je prends	J'ai pris	Je prenais	Je prendrai
Tu prends	Tu as pris	Tu prenais	Tu prendras
Il / Elle / On prend	Il / Elle / On a pris	Il / Elle / On prenait	Il / Elle / On prendr
Nous prenons	Nous avez pris	Nous prenions	Nous prendrons
Vous prenez	Vous ont pris	Vous preniez	Vous prendrez
Ils / Elles prennent	Ils / Elles ont pris	Ils / Elles prenaient	Ils / Elles prendron

To put: METTRE

Je mets	J'ai mis	Je mettais	Je mettrai
Tu mets	Tu as mis	Tu mettais	Tu mettras
Il / Elle / On met	Il / Elle / On a mis	Il / Elle / On mettait	Il / Elle / On mettra
Nous mettons	Nous avez mis	Nous mettions	Nous mettrons
Vous mettez	Vous ont mis	Vous mettiez	Vous mettrez
Ils / Elles mettent	Ils / Elles ont mis	Ils / Elles mettaient	Ils / Elles mettront

To come: VENIR

Je viens	Je suis venu (e) *	Je venais	Je viendrai
Tu viens	Tu es venu (e)	Tu venais	Tu viendras
Il / Elle / On vient	Il / Elle / On est venu (e)	Il / Elle / On venait	Il / Elle / On viendr
Nous venons	Nous sommes venu (e/s)	Nous venions	Nous viendrons
Vous venez	Vous êtes venu (e/s)	Vous veniez	Vous viendrez
Ils / Elles viennent	Ils / Elles sont venu (e/s)	Ils / Elles venaient	Ils / Elles viendront

To go out: SORTIR

Je sors	Je suis sorti (e) *	Je sortais	Je sortirais
Tu sors	Tu es sorti (e)	Tu sortais	Tu sortiras
Il / Elle / On sort	Il / Elle / On est sorti (e	Il / Elle / On sortait	Il / Elle / On sortira
Nous sortons	Nous sommes sorti (e/s)	Nous sortions	Nous sortirons
Vous sortez	Vous êtes sorti (e/s)	Vous sortiez	Vous sortirez
Ils / Elles sortent	Ils / Elles sont sorti (e/s)	Ils / Elles sortaient	Ils / Elles sortiront

*add -e for female and -s for plu

PRESENT	PASSÉ COMPOSÉ	IMPARFAIT	FUTUR

leave: PARTIR

PRESENT	PASSÉ COMPOSÉ	IMPARFAIT	FUTUR
pars	Je **suis parti (e)** *	Je **partais**	Je **partirai**
pars	Tu **es parti (e)**	Tu **partais**	Tu **partiras**
/ Elle / On **part**	Il / Elle / On **est parti (e**	Il / Elle / On **partait**	Il / Elle / On **partira**
us **partons**	Nous **sommes parti (e/s)**	Nous **partions**	Nous **partirons**
us **partez**	Vous **êtes parti (e/s)**	Vous **partiez**	Vous **partirez**
s / Elles **partent**	Ils / Elles **sont parti (e/s)**	Ils / Elles **partaient**	Ils / Elles **partiront**

feel: SENTIR

PRESENT	PASSÉ COMPOSÉ	IMPARFAIT	FUTUR
sens	J'ai **senti**	Je **sentais**	Je **sentirai**
sens	Tu **as senti**	Tu **sentais**	Tu **sentiras**
/ Elle / On **sent**	Il / Elle / On **a senti**	Il / Elle / On **sentait**	Il / Elle / On **sentira**
us **sentons**	Nous **avez senti**	Nous **sentions**	Nous **sentirons**
us **sentez**	Vous **ont senti**	Vous **sentiez**	Vous **sentirez**
s / Elles **sentent**	Ils / Elles **ont senti**	Ils / Elles **sentaient**	Ils / Elles **sentiront**

see: VOIR

PRESENT	PASSÉ COMPOSÉ	IMPARFAIT	FUTUR
vois	J'ai **vu**	Je **voyais**	Je **verrai**
vois	Tu **as vu**	Tu **voyais**	Tu **verras**
/ Elle / On **voit**	Il / Elle / On **a vu**	Il / Elle / On **voyait**	Il / Elle / On **verra**
us **voyons**	Nous **avez vu**	Nous **voyions**	Nous **verrons**
us **voyez**	Vous **ont vu**	Vous **voyiez**	Vous **verrez**
s / Elles **voient**	Ils / Elles **ont vu**	Ils/Elles **voyaient**	Ils/Elles **verront**

to drink: BOIRE

PRESENT	PASSÉ COMPOSÉ	IMPARFAIT	FUTUR
bois	J'ai **bu**	Je **buvais**	Je **boirai**
u **bois**	Tu **as bu**	Tu **buvais**	Tu **boiras**
I / Elle / On **boit**	Il / Elle / On **a bu**	Il / Elle / On **buvait**	Il / Elle / On **boira**
ous **buvons**	Nous **avez bu**	Nous **buvions**	Nous **boirons**
ous **buvez**	Vous **ont bu**	Vous **buviez**	Vous **boirez**
Ils / Elles **boivent**	Ils / Elles **ont bu**	Ils / Elles **buvaient**	Ils / Elles **boiront**

eat: MANGER

PRESENT	PASSÉ COMPOSÉ	IMPARFAIT	FUTUR
mange	J'ai **mangé**	Je **mangeais**	Je **mangerai**
manges	Tu **as mangé**	Tu **mangeais**	Tu **mangeras**
/ Elle / On **mange**	Il / Elle / On **a mangé**	Il / Elle / On **mangeait**	Il /Elle/ On **mangera**
ous **mangeons**	Nous **avez mangé**	Nous **mangions**	Nous **mangerons**
ous **mangez**	Vous **ont mangé**	Vous **mangiez**	Vous **mangerez**
s / Elles **mangent**	Ils / Elles **ont mangé**	Ils / Elles **mangeaient**	Ils / Elles **mangeront**

*add -**e** for female and -**s** for plural

Accountant	Comptable	**Bakery**	La boulangerie	**Bicycle**	Le vélo
Address	Adresse	**Balcony**	Le balcon	**Big(Fat)**	Gros/Grosse
Ads	Publicité	**Ball**	La balle/Le ballon	**Big(Tall)**	Grand(e)
Africa	Afrique (L')	**Balloons**	Les ballons	**Bill**	La facture
Airport	L'aéroport	**Banana**	La banane	**Biology**	La biologie
Aisle (store)	Le rayon	**Bandage**	Le pansement	**Bird**	L'oiseau (m.)
Alarm Clock	Le réveil	**Bank**	La banque	**Birth**	La naissance
Algebra	Algèbre	**Bank Account**	Le compte bancaire	**Birthday**	L'anniversaire (m.
Almonds	Les amandes (f.)	**Banker**	Le banquier	**Birthday Cake**	Le gâteau d'anniversaire
Alright!	D'accord!	**Bar**	Le bar	**Black**	Noir(e)
Ambulance	L'Ambulance (f.)	**Baseball**	Le baseball	**Black Pepper**	Le poivre
American	Américain(e)	**Basement**	Le sous-sol	**Black/Whiteboard**	Tableau (m.)
Amusement Park	Parc d'attraction	**Basket (shopping)**	Le panier	**Bladder**	La vessie
Angry	En colère	**Basketball**	Le basket-ball	**Blanket**	La couverture
Animal	L'Animal (m.)	**Bat**	La chauve-souris	**Blue**	Bleu(e)
Answer	La réponse	**Bathroom**	La salle de bain	**Board Game**	Le jeu de société
Ant	La Fourmi	**Bathtub**	La baignoire	**Body**	Le corps
Antarctica	Antarctique (L')	**Battery**	La pile	**Bones**	Les os (m.)
Anxious	Anxieux/se	**Be Able to/Can**	Pouvoir	**Book**	Le livre
Apartment	Appartement (m.)	**Be Bored (to)**	S'ennuyer	**Boring**	Ennuyeux/se
Appetizer	L'entrée (f.)	**Be Hired (to)**	Être embauché	**Boxer Short**	Le caleçon
Apple	La pomme	**Be Hungry (to)**	Avoir faim	**Boyfriend**	Le petit-ami
Appointment	Le rendez-vous	**Be fired (to)**	Être renvoyé	**Bra**	Le soutien-gorge
Apricot	L'abricot (m.)	**Be retired (to)**	Être envoyé	**Brain**	Le cerveau
Apron	Le tablier	**Beach**	La plage	**Brasil**	Brésil
Arcade Games	Les Jeux d'Arcade	**Beach Chair**	La chaise de plage	**Brasilian**	Brésilien(ne)
Arctic	Arctique (L')	**Beach Towel**	La serviette de	**Bread**	Le pain
Arm	Le bras		plage	**Break (to)**	Casser
Arrival	L'arrivée	**Beach Umbrella**	Le parasol	**Breakfast**	Le petit-déjeuner
Arrow	La flèche	**Beans**	Les haricots	**Brioche Bread**	La brioche
Art	L'art	**Bear**	L'ours	**Broom**	Le balai
Artist	L'artiste	**Beautiful**	Beau/Belle	**Brother**	Le frère
Asia	Asie (L')	**Beauty Salon**	Le salon de beauté	**Brother-In-Law**	Le beau-frère
Ask (to)	Demander	**Bed**	Le lit	**Brown**	Marron
ATM	Guichet automatique	**Bedroom**	La chambre	**Brush**	La brosse
Attic	Le grenier	**Bee**	L'abeille	**Bucket**	Le seau
Aunt	La tante	**Beef**	Le boeuf	**Building**	Le bâtiment
Ax	La hache	**Believe (to)**	Croire	**Bumper Cars**	Les autos-tamponneu
Baby	Le bébé	**Bell Pepper**	Le poivron	**Bunny**	Le lapin
Back	Le dos	**Belly**	Le ventre	**Buoy / Floaty**	La bouée
Backyard	Le jardin	**Belt**	La ceinture	**Burn (to)**	Brûler
Bad	Mauvais(e)	**Bench**	Le banc	**Bus**	Le bus

- Word list -

...sinessman	L'homme d'affaires	Chocolate Croissant	Le croissant au chocolat	Crocodile	Le crocodile
...tcher Shop	La boucherie			Croissant	Le croissant
...tter	Le beurre	Choose (to)	Choisir	Crow	Le corbeau
...tterfly	Le papillon	Christmas	Noël	Crowd	La foule
...y (to)	Acheter	Christmas Eve	Le réveillon de Noël	Cry (to)	Pleurer
...e!	Salut!	Church	L'église	Cucumber	Le concombre
...ke	Le gâteau	Circle	Le cercle	Curious	Curieux/se
...lculator	La calculatrice	Circus	Le cirque	Cut (to)	Couper
...ll (to)	Appeler	City	La ville	Cute	Mignon(ne)
...mera	L'appareil photo	City Hall	La mairie	Dance (to)	Dancer
...nada	Canada (Le)	Classroom	La classe	Daughter	La fille
...nadian	Canadien(ne)	Clean	Propre	Daughter-In-Law	La belle-fille
...ndies	Les bonbons (m.)	Clean (to)	Nettoyer	Death	La mort
...ndle	La bougie	Client	Le client	Debit Card	La cart bancaire
...ndy Apple	La pomme d'amour	Cliff	La falaise	Decorations	Les décorations
...r	La voiture	Closed	Fermé(e)	Delicious	Délicieux/se
...r Rental	La location de voiture	Close (it's)	Proche (c'est)	Delivery	La livraison
...rd Number	Le numéro de carte	Clothes	Les vêtements (m.)	Dentist	Le/la dentiste
...rousel	Le manège	Coat	Le manteau	Departure	Le départ
...rrot	La carotte	Cockroach	Le cafard	Desert	Le désert
...rry-On	Le bagage à main	Coffee	Le café	Desk	Le bureau
...sh Register	La caisse	Coffee Shop	Le café	Dessert	Le dessert
...shier	Le/la caissier/ère	Cold	Froid(e)	Determination	La determination
...t	Le chat	Cold (a) (Sick)	Le rhume	Different	Différent(e)
...uliflower	Le chou-fleur	Colleague	Le/La collègue	Difficult	Difficile
...real Bar	La barre de cérérales	Color	La couleur	Dining Room	La salle à manger
...arge (to)	Charger	Computer	L'ordinateur (m.)	Dinner	Le dinner
...heap/ Inexpensive	Pas cher	Concert	Le concert	Director/CEO	Le directeur
...neck (bill)	L'addition (f.)	Conditioner	L'après-shampoing	Dirty	Sale
...neck	Le chèque	Congratulations!	Félicitations	Dirty Clothes	Le linge sale
...neckbook	Le chéquier	Continent	Le continent	Discount	La remise
...neek	La joue	Cook (to)	Cuisiner	Disgusting	Dégoutant(e)
...neese	Le fromage	Cook/Chef	Le cuisinier/chef	Divorced	Divorcé(e)
...hemistry	La chimie	Cookie	Le biscuit	Do (to)	Faire
...herries	Les cerises (f.)	Corn	Le maïs	Doctor	Le médecin
...nest	La poitrine	Cotton Candy	La barbe à papa	Dog	Le chien
...hicken	Le poulet	Cough (a)	La toux	Doll	La poupée
...hildren	Les enfants	Country	Le pays	Dolphin	Le dauphin
...hin	Le menton	Couple (a)	Le couple	Donkey	L'âne
...hina	Chine (La)	Courage	Le courage	Donut	Le beignet
...hinese	Chinois(e)	Cousin	Le/la cousin(e)	Door	La porte
...hips	Les chips	Cow	La vache	Download (To)	Télécharger
...hocolate	Le chocolat	Crab	Le crab		

- Word list -

Dream	Le rêve	**Fabric Softener**	L'adoucissant	**French**	Français(e)
Dress	La robe	**Face**	Le visage	**Friend**	L'ami(e)
Drink (to)	Boire	**Fall (to)**	Tomber	**Friendly**	Sympa
Drinks	Les boissons (f.)	**Fall In Love (to)**	Tomber amoureux(se)	**Fries**	Les frites (f.)
Drops	Le gouttes (f.)			**Frog**	La grenouille
Drums	La batterie	**Family**	La famille	**Frozen Foods**	Le surgelé
Dry	Sec/sèche	**Far (it's)**	C'est loin	**Fruits**	Les fruits
Dryer	Le sèche-linge	**Farmer's Market**	Le marché	**Fun**	Amusant(e)
Duck	Le canard	**Fast**	Rapide	**Funny**	Drôle
Dust Pan	La pelle	**Father**	Le père	**Gaming Console**	La console
Eagle	L'aigle (m.)	**Father's Day**	La fête des pères	**Garage**	Le garage
Ear	L'oreille	**Father-In-Law**	Le beau-père	**Generosity**	La générosité
Early	Tôt	**Fence**	La barrière	**Geography**	La géographie
Earrings	Les boucles d'oreille	**Ferris Wheel**	La grande roue	**Geometry**	La géometrie
Earth	La Terre	**Fever**	La fièvre	**German**	Allemand(e)
East	Est	**Find (to)**	Trouver	**Germany**	Allemagne (L')
Easter	Pâques	**Finger**	Le doigt	**Get A Degree**	Obtenir un diplôn
Easy	Facile	**Finish (to)**	Finir	**Get A Job**	Obtenir un empl
Eat (to)	Manger	**Firefighter**	Le pompier	**Get Dressed**	S'habiller
Eel	L'anguille (f.)	**Fireplace**	La cheminée	**Get Married**	Se marrier
Egg	L'oeuf (m.)	**Fireworks**	Les feux d'artifice	**Get Pregnant**	Tomber enceinte
Elementary School	L'école élémentaire	**First Day Of School**	La rentrée	**Gift**	Le cadeau
Elephant	L'éléphant	**Fish**	Le poisson	**Gift Card**	La carte-cadeau
Elevator	L'ascenseur	**Fish (to)**	Pêcher	**Giraffe**	La girafe
Embarrassed	Embarrassé(e)	**Flamingo**	Le flamant rose	**Girlfriend**	La petite-amie
Embassy	L'ambassade	**Flight**	Le vol	**Give (to)**	Donner
Employee	L'employé(e)	**Floor (Ground)**	Le sol	**Glue**	La colle
Engineer	L'ingénieur(e)	**Floor (Level)**	L'étage	**Go Down (to)**	Descendre
English	Anglais (L')	**Flower Bouquet**	Le bouquet de fleurs	**Go For A Walk**	Se promener
Envelope	L'enveloppe (f.)	**Flowers**	Le fleurs (f.)	**Go Out (to)**	Sortir
Eraser	L'effaceur (m.)	**Flute/Recorder**	La flûte	**Go Straight**	Aller tout droit
Escalator	L'escalateur	**Fly (a)**	La mouche	**Go Up (to)**	Monter
Europe	Europe (L')	**Focused**	Concentré(e)	**Good**	Bon(ne)
Ex-Husband	L'ex-mari	**Food**	La nourriture	**Good day!**	Bonne journée
Ex-Wife	L'ex-femme	**Foot**	Le pied	**Good evening!**	Bonsoir
Exam	L'examen	**Football**	Le football américain	**Good night**	Bonne nuit
Excited	Enthousiaste	**Forehead**	Le front	**Goodbye!**	Au revoir
Excuse me (form.)	Excusez-moi	**Foreign Language**	La langue étrangère	**Goose**	L'oie (f.)
Excuse me (inf.)	Excuse-moi	**Forest**	La forêt	**Grades**	Les notes (f.)
Exercise	L'exercice	**Fountain**	La fontaine	**Granddaughter**	La petite-fille
Expensive	Cher/chère	**France**	France (La)	**Grandfather**	Le grand-père
Eyes	Les yeux	**Free**	Gratuit(e)	**Grandmother**	La grand-mère

- Word list -

andson	Le petit-fils	Hot Chocolate	Le chocolat chaud	Lamb	L'agneau (m.)
apes	Les raisins (m.)	Hotel	L'hôtel	Lamp	La lamp
ass	L'herbe (f.)	Hotel Room	La chambre d'hôtel	Late	En retard
atitude	La gratitude	House	La maison	Latte/Coffee With Milk	Café au lait
een	Vert(e)	How	Comment	Laugh (to)	Rire
een Beans	Les haricots verts (m.)	How are you? Comment (form./pl.) allez-vous?		Laundry/Soap	La lessive
ey	Gris(e)			Laundry Basket	Le panier à linge
ests	Les invités	How are you? (inf.)	Comment vas-tu?	Laundry Room	La buanderie
itar	La guitare	Hurricane	L'ouragan (m.)	Lawyer	L'avocat(e)
mnastics	La gymnastique	I	Je	Left	Gauche
ir	Les cheveux (m.)	I am	Je suis	Leg	La jambe
ir Salon	Le salon de coiffure	I have	J'ai	Lemon	Le citron
llway	Le couloir	Ice Cream	Le glace	Lemonade	La limonade
mmer	Le marteau	Ice Cubes	Les glaçons	Lesson	La leçon
nd	La main	Ice Skating	Le patinage	Letter	La lettre
ppy	Heureux/se	In-Laws	La belle-famille	Lettuce	La laitue
ppy Birthday!	Joyeux anniversaire	Injury	La blessure	Library	La bibliothèque
ppy Father's Day	Bonne fête des pères	Insect	L'insecte (m.)	Lion	Le lion
ppy Mother's Day	Bonne fête des mères	Instrument	L'instrument (m.)	Listen	Écouter
ppy New Year	Bonne année	Interesting	Intéressant(e)	Literature	La littérature
t	Le chapeau	Interview	L'entretien	Live (to)	Vivre
ve A Picnic	Faire un pique-niquer	Intestin	Les intestins	Liver	Le foie
ve to /Must	Devoir	Iron	Le fer à repasser	Living Room	Le salon
e	Il	Island	L'île (f.)	Lizard	Le lézard
e has	Il a	Italian	Italien(ne)	Loan	Le prêt
e is	Il est	Italy	Italie (L')	Lobster	Le homard
ad	La tête	It's	C'est	Long	Long
adache	Le mal de tête	Jacket	La veste	Loyalty	La loyauté
alth	La santé	Jam	La confiture	Lunch	Le déjeuner
ar	Entendre	Japan	Japon	Lungs	Les poumons
art	Le coeur	Japanese	Japonais(e)	Magazines	Les magazines
ello	Bonjour	Jellyfish	La méduse	Mail	Le courrier
	Salut	Jewelry	Les bijoux (m.)	Mailbox	La boîte aux lettres
gh School	Le lyçée	Juice	Le jus	Mailman	Le facteur
ppopotamus	L'hippopotame	Jupiter	Jupiter	Main Course	Le plat principal
story	L'histoire (f.)	Ketchup	Le ketchup	Mall	Le centre commercial
mework	Les devoirs (m.)	Kidneys	Les reins (m.)		
onesty	L'honnêteté	Kindness	La gentillesse	Manager	Le gérant/manager
oney	Le miel	Kitchen	La cuisine	Map	La carte
orse	Le cheval	Knee	Le genou	Married	Marié(e)
ospital	L'hôpital	Ladder	L'échelle	Mars	Mars
ot	Chaud	Lake	Le lac	Mask	Le masque

Math	Les maths	**Neptune**	Neptune	**Park (the)**	Le parc
Maybe	Peut-être	**New**	Nouv**eau/elle**	**Parking**	Le parking
Mayonnaise	La mayonnaise	**New Year's Day**	Le Nouvel An	**Parrot**	Le perroquet
Me	Moi	**New Year's Eve**	Le réveillon du	**Party**	La fête
Mean	Méchant(e)		Nouvel An	**Passport**	Le passport
Meat	La viande	**Nice to meet you**	Enchant´(e)	**Pasta**	Les pâtes
Medication	Le médicament	**Nice/Kind**	Gentil(le)	**Pastry**	La pâtisserie
Meeting	Le rendez-vous	**Niece**	La nièce	**Pastry Shop**	La pâtisserie
Menu	Le menu	**Nightclub**	La boîte de nuit	**Patience**	La patience
Mercury	Mercure	**Noodles**	Le nouilles	**Patient**	Le (la) patient(e)
Merry Christmas	Joyeux Noël	**North**	Nord	**Pay (to)**	Payer
Mexican	Mexicain(e)	**North America**	Amérique du Nord	**Peach**	La pêche
Mexico	Mexique (Le)	**Nose**	Le nez	**Peanuts**	Les cacahuètes
Middle School	Le collège	**Not bad**	Pas mal	**Pear**	La poire
Milk	Le lait	**Not very good**	Pas très bien	**Peas**	Les petits-pois
Mineral Water	L'eau minérale	**Notebook**	Le cahier	**Pedestrian Crossing**	Le passage
Mirror	Le miroir	**Number**	Le nombre		piétons
Monkey	Le singe	**Nurse**	L'infirmi**er/ère**	**Pen**	Le stylo
Moon	La lune	**Nursery**	La crèche	**Pencil**	Le crayon
Mop	La serpillère	**Nuts/Walnuts**	Les noix	**Penguin**	Le pingouin
Moroccan	Marocain(e)	**Ocean**	L'océan	**People**	Les gens
Morocco	Maroc (Le)	**Oceania**	L'Océanie	**Pharmacy**	La pharmacie
Mosque	La mosquée	**Octopus**	La pieuvre	**Physics**	La physique
Mosquito	Le moustique	**Of course!**	Bien sûr	**Piano**	Le piano
Mother	La mère	**Oil**	L'huile (f.)	**Pie**	La tarte
Mother's Day	La fête des mères	**Old**	Vieux/vieille	**Pigeon**	Le pigeon
Mother-In-Law	La belle-mère	**Olive Oil**	L'huile d'olive (f.)	**Pill**	La pillule
Motorcycle	La moto	**Omelet**	L'omelette (f.)	**Pillow**	Le coussin/
Mountain	La montagne	**Onion**	L'onion (f.)		oreiller (bed)
Mouse	La souris	**Open**	Ouvert(e)	**Pin Number /Code**	Le code PIN
Mouth	La bouche	**Orange (fruit)**	L'orange (f.)	**Pineapple**	L'ananas
Movie theater	Le cinéma	**Orange (color)**	Orange	**Ping-Pong**	Le ping-pong
Muscles	Les muscles	**Orca**	L'orque (f.)	**Pink**	Rose
Museum	Le musée	**Order (to) (food)**	Commander	**Plane**	L'avion (m.)
Mushroom	Le champignon	**Ostrich**	L'autruche (f.)	**Plane Ticket**	Le billet d'avion
Music	La musique	**Oval**	Oval	**Planet**	La planète
Musician	Le musicien(ne)	**Owl**	Le hibou	**Play (to)**	Jouer
Mustard	La moutarde	**Oyster**	L'huître	**Playground**	L'aire de jeu
Neck	Le cou	**Package (in mail)**	Le colis	**Pleasant**	Agréable
Necklace	Le collier	**Pain**	La douleur	**Please (form.)**	S'il vous plaît
Neighbor	Le (la) voisin(e	**Panties**	Les sous-vêtements	**Please (inf.)**	S'il te plaît
Neighborhood	Le quartier	**Pants**	Le pantalon	**Police Station**	La station de police
Nephew	Le neveu			**Policeman**	Le policier

- Word list -

r	Pauvre	**Roller Coaster**	Les montagnes russes	**Sheep**	Le mouton
k	Le porc	**Roof**	Le toit	**Sheet Of Paper**	La feuille de papier
t Office	Le bureau de poste	**Rope**	La corde	**Shirt**	La chemise
tcard	La carte postale	**Ruler**	La règle	**Shoes**	Les chaussures
ato	La pomme de terre	**Run (to)**	Courir	**Shop (to)**	Faire du shopping
ær Drill	La perceuse électrique	**Sad**	Triste	**Shopping Cart**	Le caddie
pare (to)	Préparer	**Salad**	La salade	**Shops (small)**	Les boutiques
school	La maternelle	**Salad Dressing**	La vinaigrette	**Short (a)**	Le short
scription	L'ordonnance	**Salary**	Le salaire	**Short (size)**	Court
ter	L'imprimante	**Sales** (seasonal discount)	Les soldes	**Shot/Injection**	La piqûre
ducts	Les produits	**Salesperson**	Vendeur/se	**Shoulder**	L'épaule
ılic Holiday	Le jour férié	**Salt**	Le sel	**Shower (A)**	La douche
lding	Le pudding	**Sand**	Le sable	**Shower (To)**	Se doucher
ple	Violet	**Sandbox**	Le bac à sable	**Shrimp**	La crevette
se	Le sac à main	**Saturn**	Saturne	**Sickness**	La maladie
amid	La pyramide	**Sauce (Hot)**	La sauce piquante	**Signature**	La signature
se Children (To)	Élever des enfants	**Saw**	La scie	**Similar**	Similaire
ɪor	Le rasoir	**Saxophone**	Le saxophone	**Sing**	Chanter
ıd (to)	Lire	**Scared (to be)**	Avoir peur	**Single**	Célibataire
ıd A Book	Lire un livre	**Scarf**	L'écharpe	**Sister**	La soeur
:eipt	Le reçu	**Science**	La science	**Sister-In-Law**	La belle-soeur
:tangle	Le rectangle	**Scissors**	Les ciseaux	**Skiing**	Faire du ski
l	Rouge	**Scorpion**	Le scorpion	**Skin**	La peau
ax (to)	Se relaxer	**Scrambled Eggs**	Les oeufs brouillés	**Skirt**	La jupe
air (to)	Réparer	**Scream (to)**	Crier	**Sleep (to)**	Dormir
ipect	Le respect	**Screw (a)**	La vis	**Slide**	Le toboggan
iponsibility	La responsabilité	**Screwdriver**	Le tourne-vis	**Slow**	Lent(e)
it (to)	Se reposer	**Sea**	La mer	**Small**	Petit(e)
itaurant	Le restaurant	**Seafood**	Les fruits de mer	**Smart**	Intelligent(e)
itrooms	Les toilettes	**Seal**	Le phoque	**Smoothie**	Le smoothie
irement	La retraite	**Secretary**	Le (la) secrétaire	**Snack**	Le goûter
noceros	Le rhinocéros	**Security Agent**	L'agent de sécurité	**Snake**	Le serpent
ɔmbus	Le losange	**See (to)**	Voir	**Snow**	La neige
e	Le riz	**See you (soon)!**	A bientôt!	**Soap**	Le savon
h	Riche	**See you later!**	À plus tard!	**Soccer**	Le foot/football
le A Bike	Faire du vélo	**Sell (to)**	Vendre	**Socks**	Les chaussettes (f.)
ght	Droite	**Serious**	Sérieux/se	**Soda**	La boisson gazeuse
ıg	La bague	**Shampoo**	Le shampoing	**Solar System**	Le système solaire
er	La rivière	**Shark**	Le requin	**Son**	Le fils
bot	Le robot	**She**	Elle	**Son-In-Law**	Le beau-fils
ck (Big)	Les pierres (f.)	**She has**	Elle a	**Sore Throat**	Le mal de gorge
ller Blading	Faire du roller	**She is**	Elle est	**Sorry!**	Désolé!

- Word list -

Soup	La soupe	**Sweater**	Un pull	**Towel (kitchen)**	La serviette
South	Sud	**Swim (to)**	Nager	**Toy**	Le jouet
South America	Amérique du Sud (L.)	**Swimming (sport)**	La natation	**Traffic Lights**	Les feux d'intersec
Space	L'espace	**Swimming Pool**	La piscine	**Train**	Le train
Spain	Espagne	**Swimsuit**	Le maillot de bain	**Tramway**	Le tramway
Spanish	Espagnol(e)	**Swing (the)**	La balançoire	**Trapezoid**	Le trapèze
Sparkly Water	L'eau gazeuse	**Synagogue**	La synagogue	**Travel (To)**	Voyager
Speak/Talk (to)	Parler	**Syrup**	Le syrop	**Travel (a)**	Un voyage
Sphere	La sphère	**T-Shirt**	Le t-shirt	**Tree**	L'arbre
Spider	L'araignée	**Take**	Prendre	**Triangle**	Le triangle
Square	Le carré	**Talk on the phone**	Parler au téléphone	**Truck**	Le camion
Squid	Le calamar	**Talk/Chitchat**	Discuter	**Trumpet**	La trompette
Squirrel	L'écureuil	**Tape (scotch tape)**	Le scotch	**Trust**	La confiance
Stairs	Les escaliers	**Taxi**	Le taxi	**Tuna**	Le thon
Stamp	Le timbre	**Tea**	Le thé	**Turkey (a)**	La dinde
Star	L'étoile	**Teacher**	Le(la) professeur(e)	**Turkey (country)**	Turquie (La)
Start	Commencer	**Teeth**	Les dents (f.)	**Turn Left**	Tourner à gauche
Station	La station	**Temple**	Le temple	**Turn Right**	Tourner à droite
Stomach	L'estomac	**Tennis**	Le tennis	**Turtle**	La tortue
Stomachache	Mal au ventre	**Thank you**	Merci	**U-Turn**	Le demi-tour
Stop (to)	Arrêter	**very much (a lot)**	(beaucoup)	**Ugly**	Moche
Store	Le magasin	**They (f.)**	Elles	**Uncle**	L'oncle
Straw	La paille	**They (m./mix)**	Ils	**Unemployment**	Le chômage
Strawberry	La fraise	**They are (f.)**	Elles sont	**United Kingdom**	Le Royaume-Un
Street	La rue	**They are (m. or mix)**	Ils sont	**United States**	Les États-Unis
Stressful	Stréssant(e)	**They have (f.)**	Elles ont	**University**	L'université
Strict	Strict(e)	**They have (m./mix)**	Ils ont	**Uranus**	Uranus
Stroller	La poucette	**Think (to)**	Penser	**Vacuum**	L'aspirateur
Strong	Fort(e)	**Ticket**	Le ticket	**Vegetables**	Les légumes
Student (Child)	Élève	**Ticket Booth**	Le guichet	**Veins**	Les veines (f.)
Student (teen +)	Étudiant(e)	**Tie (the)**	La cravate	**Venus**	Vénus
Stuffed Animal	La peluche	**Tiger**	Le tigre	**Very good**	Très bien
Stupid	Stupid / bête	**Tip (the)**	Le pourboire	**Video Game**	Le jeu vidéo
Subway	Le métro	**Toast (the)**	La tartine	**Violin**	Le violon
Suit (outfit)	Le costume	**Toilet Paper**	Le papier toilet	**Volcano**	Le volcan
Suitcase	La valise (Le bagage)	**Tolerance**	La tolérance	**Volleyball**	Le volley-ball
Sunglasses	Le lunettes de soleil	**Tomato**	La tomate	**Waffle**	La gaufre
Sunny Side Up Eggs	Les oeufs aux plat	**Tongue**	La langue	**Wait (To)**	Attendre
Sunscreen	L'écran solaire	**Tool**	L'outil	**Waiter**	Le (la) serveur/se
Supermarket	Le supermarché	**Toothbrush**	La brosse à dents	**Wake Up**	Se réveiller
Surgery	La chirurgie	**Toothpaste**	Le dentifrice	**Walk (To)**	Marcher
Surprised	Surpris(e)	**Tourist**	La (la) touriste		

- Word list -

lk The Dog	Promener le chien	You're welcome	De rien	37	Trente-sept
ll	Le mur	Young	Jeune	38	Trente-huit
sh (To)	Laver	Zebra	Le zèbre	39	Trente-neuf
sher	La machine à laver	Zoo	Le zoo	40	Quarante
tch Tv (To)	Regarder la télé	Zucchini	La courgette	41	Quarante et un
ter	L'eau	0	Zéro	42	Quarante-deux
terfall	La cascade	1	Un	43	Quarante-trois
termelon	La pastèque	2	Deux	44	Quarante-quatre
ve (the)	La vague	3	Trois	45	Quarante-cinq
(form.)	Nous	4	Quatre	46	Quarante-six
(informal)	On	5	Cinq	47	Quarante-sept
are (form.)	Nous sommes	6	Six	48	Quarante-huit
are (inf.)	On est	7	Sept	49	Quarante-neuf
have (form.)	Nous avons	8	Huit	50	Cinquante
have (inf.)	On a	9	Neuf	51	Cinquante et un
ak	Faible	10	Dix	52	Cinquante-deux
dding	Le mariage	11	Onze	53	Cinquante-trois
ight Training	La musculation	12	Douze	54	Cinquante-quatre
st	Ouest	13	Treize	55	Cinquante-cinq
t	Mouillé	14	Quatorze	56	Cinquante-six
ale	La baleine	15	Quinze	57	Cinquante-sept
ite	Blanc(che)	16	Seize	58	Cinquante-huit
dow	La veuve	17	Dix-sept	59	Cinquante-neuf
dower	Le veuf	18	Dix-huit	60	Soixante
nter	L'hiver	19	Dix-neuf	61	Soixante et un
re Transfer	Le virement	20	Vingt	62	Soixante-deux
lf	Le loup	21	Vingt et un	63	Soixante-trois
ods	Les bois	22	Vingt-deux	64	Soixante-quatre
rk (to)	Travailler	23	Vingt-trois	65	Soixante-cinq
rld	Le monde	24	Vingt-quatre	66	Soixante-six
ite	Écrire	25	Vingt-cinq	67	Soixante-sept
Ray	La radio(graphie)	26	Vingt-six	68	Soixante-huit
llow	Jaune	27	Vingt-sept	69	Soixante-neuf
s / No	Oui/Non	28	Vingt-huit	70	Soixante-dix
gurt	Le yaourt	29	Vingt-neuf	71	Soixante et onze
u (Plur.)	Vous	30	Trente	72	Soixante-douze
u (form.)	Vous	31	Trente et un	73	Soixante-treize
u (inf.)	Tu	32	Trente-deux	74	Soixante-quatorze
u are (in.)	Tu es	33	Trente-trois	75	Soixante-quinze
u are (form. Or group)	Vous êtes	34	Trente-quatre	76	Soixante-seize
u have (form.)	Vous avez	35	Trente-cinq	77	Soixante-dix-sept
u have (inf.)	Tu as	36	Trente-six	78	Soixante-dix-huit

79	Soixante-dix-neuf
80	Quatre-vingts
81	Quatre-vingt-un
82	Quatre-vingt-deux
83	Quatre-vingt-trois
84	Quatre-vingt-quatre
85	Quatre-vingt-cinq
86	Quatre-vingt-six
87	Quatre-vingt-sept
88	Quatre-vingt-huit
89	Quatre-vingt-neuf
90	Quatre-vingt-dix
91	Quatre-vingt-onze
92	Quatre-vingt-douze
93	Quatre-vingt-treize
94	Quatre-vingt-quatorze
95	Quatre-vingt-quinze
96	Quatre-vingt-seize
97	Quatre-vingt-dix-sept
98	Quatre-vingt-dix-huit
99	Quatre-vingt-dix-neuf
100	Cent
101	Cent un
102	Cent deux
103...	Cent trois
200	Deux cent**s**
205	Deux cent cinq
220	Deux cent vingt
637	Six cent trente-sept
708	Sept cent huit
999	Neuf cent quatre-vingt-dix-neuf
1,000	Mille
2023	Deux mille vingt-trois
2024	Deux mille vingt-quatre
7,600	Sept mille six cents
10,000	Dix mille
50,000	Cinquante mille
100,000	Cent mille
1,000,000	Un million
1,000,000,000	Un milliard

Made in the USA
Las Vegas, NV
13 November 2023

80731165R00131